THE

G000081327

Ronald Hamilton was born i
ter College and at Magdalene College, Cambridge. He has been
a schoolmaster for most of his civilian life, first at Bromsgrove
School and then at Winchester College, where he taught
history and modern languages for twenty-five years, and was a
house master for eighteen. During the war years (1939-46) he
served in the Intelligence Corps in Europe, the Middle East,
India and Burma, reaching the rank of colonel and receiving
the OBE. He married in 1958 and now lives in Gloucestershire.

Ronald Hamilton wrote *A Holiday History of Scotland* after
the successful publication by Chatto & Windus of *Now I
Remember: A Holiday History of England* (1964) and *A Holiday
History of France* (1971). All three titles in the series are now
available, in updated paperback editions, from The Hogarth
Press.

By the same author

FREDERICK THE GREAT
PENDLEBURY AND THE PLASTER SAINTS
(with Colin Badcock)
BUDGE FIRTH: A Memoir and Some Sermons
(editor and part author)
NOW I REMEMBER:
A Holiday History of England
A HOLIDAY HISTORY OF FRANCE
SUMMER PILGRIMAGE
THE PLUSCARDEN STORY

A HOLIDAY
HISTORY
OF
SCOTLAND

Ronald Hamilton

THE HOGARTH PRESS

LONDON

for
BID and DUNCAN
who started me off on the banks
of
the Findhorn

Published in 1986 by
The Hogarth Press
Chatto and Windus Ltd
40 William IV Street, London WC2N 4DF

First published in Great Britain by Chatto & Windus 1975
Hogarth edition offset, with additions, from original Chatto edition
Copyright © Ronald Hamilton 1975, 1986

British Library in Publication Data

Hamilton, Ronald
A holiday history of Scotland
1. Scotland – History
I. Title
941.1   DA760

ISBN 0 7012 0698 5

Printed in Great Britain by
Redwood Burn
Trowbridge, Wiltshire

THE OBJECT

If you are going to get any enjoyment, or value, out of this book, you must understand the object with which it has been written. The object is to enliven your sight-seeing by providing you with the historical background to which guide-books can, inevitably, devote little space.

THIS IS NOT A GUIDE-BOOK. IT IS DESIGNED TO SUPPLEMENT YOUR GUIDE-BOOK.

Perhaps you have looked at a church, or castle, a house or a work of art (the date of which you have been told) and have said to yourself: "I wish I could remember what was happening when this was built or that was made." This is where your *Holiday History* comes in – NOT as what has been described as "a long fireside pipe-and-slipper read" but, I hope, as a handy work of reference for the enquiring traveller in Scotland.

It is divided into nine periods, each of which is preceded by a short note giving an indication of the period's sight-seeing potentialities. Within these divisions Scottish history unrolls itself reign by reign. This method is used because the traveller is continually being driven back to Kings, Queens and dates: "David I founded this monastery, Alexander II built that castle, here died Robert III, James V embellished this palace, Mary Queen of Scots lay ill here." Some of these monarchs may be shadowy figures to some of you.

So I hope you'll throw the book into the car or stuff it in your rucksack. If it helps to answer some of your own or your children's questions, and thus makes your holiday the happier, it will have done what it set out to do.

RONALD HAMILTON

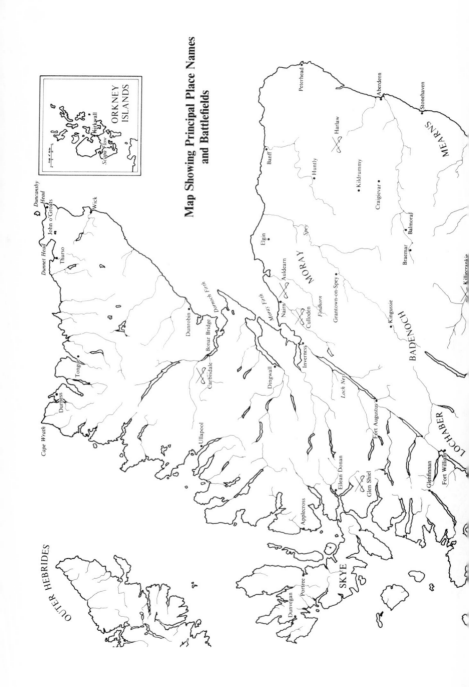

Map Showing Principal Place Names and Battlefields

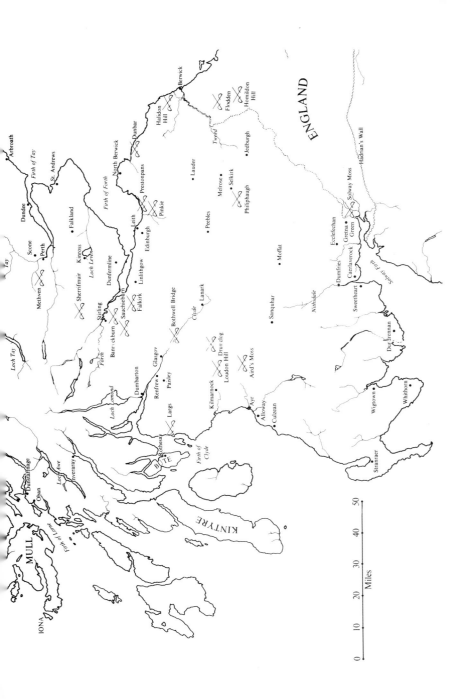

ENGLAND

Arbroath

Firth of Tay

Dundee

St. Andrews

Tay

Scone

Perth

Falkland

Methven

Kinross

Sherrifmuir

Loch Leven

Dunfermline

Firth of Forth

North Berwick

Leith

Edinburgh

Dunbar

Preston pans

Pinkie

Linlithgow

Stirling

Bannockburn

Sauchieburn

Falkirk

Forth

Bothwell Bridge

Lanark

Clyde

Dumbarton

Glasgow

Renfrew

Paisley

Kilmarnock

Drumclog

Loudon Hill

Aird's Moss

Largs

Ayr

Alloway

Culzean

Berwick

Halidon Hill

Flodden

Homildon Hill

Tweed

Jedburgh

Lauder

Melrose

Selkirk

Philiphaugh

Peebles

Moffat

Sanquhar

Ecclefechan

Dumfries

Caerlaverock

Gretna Green

Solway Moss

Hadrian's Wall

Solway Firth

Nithsdale

Sweetheart

Dundrennan

Wigtown

Whithorn

Stranraer

Loch Tay

Loch Lomond

Firth of Clyde

Rothesay

BUTE

KINTYRE

MULL

IONA

Dunstaffnage

Oban

Loch Awe

Inveraray

Firth of Lorne

0   10   20   30   40   50

Miles

Contents

Acknowledgments

The sources of the photographic illustrations in this book are all acknowledged individually, and I am grateful to those who have given me permission to reproduce them.

The line drawings illustrating reigns are the work of Miss T. Ritchie, who prepared them specially for this volume.

I wish to express my thanks for being allowed to quote from the following:

Puck of Pook's Hill by Rudyard Kipling. (By permission of Mrs George Bambridge, Macmillan Co. of London and Basingstoke, and Macmillan Co. of Canada.)

A Summer in Skye by Alexander Smith. (Quoted from *A Book of Scotland*, edited by G. F. Maine. Collins.)

A Short History of Scotland by Robert L. Mackie. (By permission of The Clarendon Press, Oxford.)

In Search of Scotland by H. V. Morton. (Methuen & Co. Ltd.)

Culross. A Short Guide to the Royal Burgh. (The National Trust for Scotland.)

I have, on occasion, been able to check points, only partially explained elsewhere, from *Scottish Kings 1005–1625* by Sir Archibald H. Dunbar, Bart. (David Douglas).

I have received much encouragement and practical assistance from friends: Mr and Mrs Duncan Mackintosh (to whom this book is dedicated); the Dunlop family at Stevenson House, Haddington; the late Brigadier Ernest Montgomery and Mrs Montgomery; Mrs John Watson and Mr Geoffrey Martin.

I am deeply indebted to the National Trust for Scotland for its good offices in putting at my disposal the fruits of great experience. I wish to express particular gratitude to two consultants whose advice is always at the disposal of the Trust, Dr Jean Munro and Mr Schomberg Scott, and to Sir James Stormonth Darling, its Director.

I am very grateful to the Scottish Tourist Board for allowing me to quote their estimated figures of visitors to Scotland during the year 1984 and for permission to end this book on a phrase of their invention.

Above all I have valued the help of Mr E. J. Cowan of the

Department of Scottish History in the University of Edinburgh, who has read my manuscript and made many helpful suggestions; of Miss Bartlett who typed it, and of my wife, thanks to whose indefatigable driving I have been able to visit by car almost every place mentioned in this book.

R.H.

For help in the preparation of this new edition, I wish to express my gratitude to: John Julius Norwich, for the caption under the Burrell Collection illustration; the Scottish Development Agency; the Industry Department for Scotland; the Scottish Information Office; the Scotch Whisky Association; and, once more, to the Scottish Tourist Board.

I wish also to thank my friends Mr David Black and Mr Charles Walmsley for valuable information and advice.

R.H., 1985

THE MINGLING OF THE PEOPLES

St Martin's Cross, Iona
(*By courtesy of the Iona Community*)

THE MINGLING OF THE PEOPLES
A.D. 80–1034

The introductory chapter which follows deals briefly with the years A.D. 80 to 1034. Thus it does not help you with the Neolithic, Bronze and Iron ages. Your guide-book, however, will direct you to quantities of chambered cairns, standing stones, stone circles, forts, brochs and duns. Particularly important among brochs is the ancient fortified place on the Shetland island of Mousa.

Of course many of these survived, and indeed their construction continued, after the Romans came, driving north with their straight-line roads. It is with the advent of Agricola (Governor of Britain from A.D. 78 to 84) that the historical background provided here begins. There are plenty of Roman remains in Scotland and you may find interest in the relics of defences which once linked Clyde and Forth (the so-called Antonine "Wall" – almost the last remnant of the outer perimeter of the Roman Empire visible today). These are worth your inspection, particularly if you are already familiar with Hadrian's Wall from the Solway to the Tyne.

The years after the Roman withdrawal offer you a wide variety of antiquities from Pictish sculptured stones (which, like brochs, are unique to Scotland) to the spate of early monastic sites and Celtic crosses which Christianity brought. Among Pictish sculptured stones there are splendid examples collected in the museum at Meigle, quite close to Glamis on the road between Perth and Forfar, and at Aberlemno, 6 miles south-west of Brechin. Among the early protagonists of Christianity St Ninian, operating in the fourth and early fifth centuries, will draw you to Whithorn (south of Wigtown), St Kentigern (or Mungo, sixth century) to Glasgow and St Columba to Iona, where he landed in A.D. 563.

Much destruction was, characteristically, wrought by the Norsemen, but they have their memorials in dwellings, artistic objects, etc. With the opening of the eleventh century we find the famous round towers of Abernethy and Brechin (of Irish provenance). Meanwhile Dumbarton's great rock had been fortified for about five hundred years.

Aerial View of the Antonine Wall, Rough Castle
(One mile east of Bonnybridge)

(Crown Copyright: reproduced by permission of the Department of the Environment)

THE MINGLING OF THE PEOPLES

From the Romans to A.D. 1034

GEOGRAPHY

Lord Chesterfield, whose wisdom still enchants devotees of elegance and order, wrote to his son in February 1750: "Never read History without having maps . . . lying by you, and constantly recurred to." So take a map of Scotland, a ruler and a pencil, and draw two west–east lines. The southern line should run from Turnberry to Dunbar, the northern from Alexandria on Loch Lomond to Aberdeen. You have now divided Scotland, like Gaul, into three parts: the Southern Uplands, the Central Lowlands and the Highlands. (Remember, however, that though it is convenient to project the Highland Line to Aberdeen, the coastal belt north of that city, as far as Nairn on the Moray Firth, is emphatically Lowland in character.) As time goes on the influence of this geographical configuration upon the history of the country will become clear.

THE ROMANS

And since Gaul has inevitably brought the Romans to mind, you will recall that there are advantages in having been forced to submit to their discipline. On the other hand there is also distinction in the presentation of a nut too hard for the Roman sledgehammer to crack – and such a nut was Scotland, whose fierce inhabitants were ready to defend, and eager to attack from, their brochs, duns and hill forts. That able and dynamic expansionist Agricola, Governor of Britain from A.D. 78 to 84, pushed forward north of the Tay in the year 81. On the unidentified battlefield of Mons Graupius (from which, in mistaken derivation, the Grampian Mountains take their name) he defeated Calgacus, leader of the Picts, in A.D. 84. Agricola's son-in-law, Tacitus, has assured Calgacus' immortality by attributing to him one of the greatest phrases in historical literature: "solitudinem faciunt, pacem appellant" (they make a desert and call it peace).

But this peace could not be maintained, despite the "line of military stations" left by Agricola to link Clyde and Forth, and, during the second decade of the second century A.D., northern troubles culminated in the sinister and total disappearance from the Roman Order of Battle of the Ninth Legion, stationed at York. A new strategy was needed and supplied by the Emperor Hadrian in A.D. 122 – during his visit to Britain – resulting in the great wall which joins Solway to Tyne across seventy-three miles of what Kipling's Parnesius, in *Puck of Pook's Hill*, described as "that big purple heather country of broken stone". Some twenty years later, under the Emperor Antoninus Pius, the legate Lollius Urbicus pushed forward and refortified Agricola's Clyde–Forth defences, but it became clear in practice that Hadrian's concept of the northern limit was the correct one. It is true that in A.D. 209 the Emperor Septimius Severus planned, and indeed attempted to start, a conquest – but his death in 211 put an end to the project. And now "the masters of the fairest and most wealthy climates of the globe turned with contempt from gloomy hills assailed by the winter tempest, from lakes concealed in a blue mist, and from cold and lonely heaths, over which the deer of the forest were chased by a troop of naked barbarians" (Gibbon). Penetration beyond what we loosely call "The Roman Wall" was, henceforth, limited to patrolling, until the legions left Britain for good in A.D. 410.

FOUR KINGDOMS

For a time this "blue mist" may be allowed to cover the North. Let it clear again during the second half of the sixth century, to reveal a new picture. By then four kingdoms had developed. From the coastal line – Cape Wrath to John o'Groats – down to Lollius Urbicus' Antonine Wall the land, except for a western enclave, was dominated by the Picts – a name ("Picti", the painted men) used by the Romans to designate, generally, the northern tribes. The enclave, known as Dalriada, was inhabited by the Scots. These, from whom Scotland was to derive her name, had emigrated from the original Dalriada, situated in the north eastern corner of Ireland (County Antrim). They had settled and fought

Slab carved with the figure of a bull (Burghead, near Elgin)
believed to be of Pictish origin

(By courtesy of the Trustees of the British Museum)

to consolidate their holding which, by the seventh century,
comprised the mainland and islands of Argyll, together with Bute
and Arran. South of the Picts, on the eastern side, were the
Angles – Teutons, these, and mainly from the Elbe estuary. Their
influence extended into what we would now call Northumberland.
To their west, driven thither by all these pressures, were the
Britons, whose area was called Strathclyde and reached south
into Cumberland.

CHRISTIANITY

And Christianity had come. Saint Ninian (c. 360–c. 432 A.D.), with experience of Rome behind him and the reputed friendship of Saint Martin of Tours to recommend him, founded a small monastery at Whithorn, south of Wigtown, the famous *Candida Casa* or White House, from which seat of godliness and good learning (subsequently an important pilgrimage centre) he and his brethren went out to convert both Britons and Picts.

Rather more than one hundred years later Ninian was followed by Saint Kentigern, honoured affectionately to this day in Glasgow as "Saint Mungo" (beloved friend) and said to have been of princely birth. Among other attractive legends it is recounted that Kentigern survived the pre-natal shock of his mother's being hurled down from Traprain Law, a hill near Haddington rich in archaeological interest, after which she drifted in an open boat to the northern bank of the Forth, landed at Culross and gave birth to her son. Here the boy studied under Saint Serf, thus qualifying himself for the evangelization of Dumfriesshire, Galloway and the Glasgow area – perhaps penetrating even further north – to die, eventually, in 603.

A character of exceptional power now makes his entrance. Saint Columba was an Irish noble, born in 521. He studied under Saint Finnian of Moville, on the shore of Strangford Lough, and subsequently sat at the feet of the other Saint Finnian at Clonnard, almost the central point of his native land. A man of religious enthusiasm and genuine sanctity; a scholar, planner, administrator and leader – it was not for nothing that he called his monks "soldiers of Christ". At the end of the eighth century there were to be no less than 795 religious houses in Ireland – these were largely the fruit of Columba's organizational labours in the middle of the sixth century.

But Columba, with all his virtues, was a passionate man. During his studies at Moville he had copied the manuscript of a rare gospel. Dispute arose about the ownership of this transcription and the saint was infuriated when the contemporary king – Diarmit, at Tara – ruled that it should belong to the possessor of the original. This fracas was followed by a quarrel about rights of

The Monymusk Reliquary, once said to have
contained bones of St. Columba

(National Museum of Antiquities of Scotland)

sanctuary and the whole affair culminated in a bloody battle for
which a synod held Columba to be responsible. Thus it became
desirable, on more than one score, that he should leave Ireland,
and, sailing with the traditional twelve companions, he landed on
Iona on the shingle of a rock-girt bay in the year 563. Dr Johnson,
traversing Mull on horseback rather more than twelve hundred
years later, found it "a most dolorous country", but, on reaching
Columba's "illustrious island", wrote what Boswell calls "this
sublime passage": "That man is little to be envied, whose
patriotism would not gain force upon the plain of *Marathon*, or
whose piety would not grow warmer among the ruins of *Iona*."

Iona, one of the brightest stars in the constellation of Celtic
Christianity, shot its rays north, east and south. Brude, King of

the Picts – a major menace to Dalriada – was apparently converted, and by degrees other fierce northerners followed his
example, influenced not only by Columba's monks but also by
his contemporary Saint Moluag. And soon it becomes apparent
that these essentially monastic missions represent an important
factor in politics as well as a powerful exercise in evangelization.
Columba was connected with the royal house of Dalriada and
struck a decisive blow for its future when, in 574, he engineered
the accession of a capable ruler in the person of that Aidan from
whom spring the Celtic kings of Scotland whose blood ran in the
veins of James VI and I.

(It would be agreeable to believe that Aidan was consecrated
on the lump of freestone traditionally called the "Black Stone of
Iona" which is held by some to have served as a pillow for the
patriarch Jacob and subsequently to have found its way from
Bethel via Egypt, Spain, Ireland, Iona, Dunstaffnage and Scone
to its resting place under the seat of Edward I's coronation chair
at Westminster.)

After Columba's death, which took place in 597, the torch was
carried by Saint Maelrubba of Applecross, Saint Aidan – the
Iona monk who become Bishop of Lindisfarne (635) – and Saint
Cuthbert, who died in 687 and who is still venerated in Durham.

Meanwhile, away in the South, in that very year 597, Saint
Augustine had arrived at Canterbury. The Romans may have
failed to subdue the country which we now call Scotland, but
eventually the Celtic church had to bow before the Papacy – "the
ghost of the deceased Roman Empire sitting crowned on the
grave thereof" (Hobbes). The process was started at the Synod of
Whitby in 664, when King Oswy of Northumbria ruled in favour
of Rome's style of tonsure and date of Easter – but many years
passed before the Pope's supremacy could be said to be complete.

THE NORSEMEN

Celtic Christianity had, obviously, been a factor working
towards unity in the North, but there is no unifier known to
History so compelling as the enemy at the gate, and the late
eighth century saw his arrival. The Anglo-Saxon Chronicle's

Model of Viking Ship (ninth century)

(The National Maritime Museum, London)

account of the year 793 sends a chill down the spine: "This year came dreadful fore-warnings over the land of the Northumbrians, terrifying the people most woefully; there were immense sheets of light rushing through the air, and whirlwinds, and fiery dragons flying across the firmament. These tremendous tokens were soon followed by a great famine; and not long after . . . the harrowing inroads of heathen men made lamentable havoc in the church of God in Holy Island, by rapine and slaughter." Thus the Norse pirates, driving west from Scandinavia, raided Lindisfarne. Next year they were at Iona. In the following century they established themselves in Shetland, Orkney, the Hebrides, in Sutherland and in Caithness. During this period of Viking settlement the relics of Saint Columba were dispersed to Dunkeld and to Kells, crosses stood deserted, while ornaments and exquisite manuscripts were spirited away to bear witness, eventually, in museums and college libraries, to a culture which will never lose its power to delight. And, though Iona long remained the burial ground of kings, there arose on the east coast another great ecclesiastical centre, said to be privileged in possessing the bones of the Apostle Saint Andrew, from whom it took its name and in whom Scotland found her patron saint.

KENNETH MAC ALPIN, MALCOLM II

Thus, by the middle of the ninth century, the situation seemed unpromising, but a King of Dalriada, Kenneth MacAlpin by name, saw a way to exploit it. He defeated the Picts, no doubt because this group of tribes had already been weakened by the depredations of the Norsemen, and was able to rule both their territory and his from 843 until his death in 858. Yet the history of the next one hundred and fifty years is troubled and savage with "many a carcass . . . left to the carrion". Nonetheless Malcolm II, King of the Picts and Scots from 1005 to 1034, found a friend and son-in-law in Sigurd, the Norse Earl of Orkney, and became guardian of the latter's infant offspring, Thorfinn, when the Earl departed to Ireland in 1014. The Norseman's timely death in battle enabled Malcolm to force vassal status upon Thorfinn, as ruler of Sutherland and Caithness, thus temporarily securing the northern front. Four years later he struck south and expanded his territories as far as the Tweed by defeating an army despatched by England's formidable King Canute at Carham, twenty miles inland from Berwick, in 1018. The year brought another stroke of good fortune in that the ruler of Strathclyde died sonless and the heritage was successfully claimed by Malcolm's grandson Duncan. Thus, when Duncan succeeded Malcolm in 1034, although the Norsemen held Shetland, Orkney, Caithness, Sutherland, the Hebrides and Argyll, Duncan ruled over something like a loosely united Scotland.

LINDISFARNE

THE CONSOLIDATION
OF THE KINGDOM
1034–1214

Duncan I	1034–1040
Macbeth	1040–1057
(Lulach	1057–1058)
Malcolm III (Canmore)	1058–1093
Donald Bane	1093–1097
(Duncan II	1094)
Edgar	1097–1107
Alexander I	1107–1124
David I	1124–1153
Malcolm IV (The Maiden)	1153–1165
William I (The Lion)	1165–1214

In England		*In France*	
Canute	1016–1035	Henry I	1031–1060
Harold I	1035–1040	Philip I	1060–1108
Hardicanute	1040–1042	Louis VI	
Edward the Confessor	1042–1066	(The Fat)	1108–1137
Harold II	1066	Louis VII	
William the Conqueror	1066–1087	(The Young)	1137–1180
William II (Rufus)	1087–1100	Philip II	
Henry I (Beauclerc)	1100–1135	(Augustus)	1180–1223
Stephen	1135–1154		
Henry II	1154–1189		
Richard I (Coeur de Lion)	1189–1199		
John (Lackland)	1199–1216		

The Cathedral of St Magnus, Kirkwall (Orkney)

(*The Scottish Field*)

THE CONSOLIDATION
OF THE KINGDOM

1034–1214

This period is, first and foremost, enormously rich in ecclesiastical foundations. There are still some dim traces of the early Culdee communities (see pages 33, 34) which faded in face of the reforms introduced by St Margaret, Queen of Malcolm Canmore, and you will find Romanesque building in the Border country, and as far north as Birnie, near Elgin, and away at Kirkwall in Orkney, where twelfth-century Norsemen raised the great cathedral of St Magnus. The lovely Border abbeys were founded by David I between 1128 and 1152 while, at parish level, the churches of Dalmeny, near Edinburgh, and Leuchars, near St Andrews, date from the same period. You will not, of course, expect to find the architectural styles of all these buildings confined to those of the eleventh, twelfth and early thirteenth centuries – there has been too much destruction and rebuilding for that – but this is when they were started.

It is, also, a great age for strongholds of the motte and bailey type. A "motte" is a mound of earth (man-made, like a child's sandcastle) with a flattened top originally surmounted by wooden fortifications. It dominated a palisaded enclosure called a bailey, to which it was attached. A spectacular late twelfth-century motte is to be found at Inverurie – on the road running north-west from Aberdeen to Huntly. By the middle of the twelfth century, however, the earliest stone castles were beginning to rise (e.g. Castle Sween, on the eastern shore of Loch Sween, opposite Jura).

These developments bear witness to the Norman infiltration of Scotland (which included monks and masons as well as magnates) – a historical process which will, perhaps, become clear in the pages which follow.

DVNCANVS. I.

Duncan I, by Jacob de Witt (or de Wett)
(*Reproduced by Gracious Permission of Her Majesty the Queen*)

"Jacob de Wett was a Dutch painter, who worked at Holyrood Palace between 1674 and 1686, and there painted the series of apocryphal portraits of the Scottish kings."

(*Bryan's Dictionary of Painters and Engravers*)

DUNCAN I, 1034–1040

(Son of Crinan the Thane, lay abbot of Dunkeld, and Bethoc, daughter of MALCOLM II. Grandson of MALCOLM II)

Born about 1001, was about 33 when he ascended the throne and, perhaps, about 39 when he was killed.

Married a cousin of Siward, Earl of Northumbria, and had two sons:

MALCOLM III (CANMORE)
DONALD BANE

Thumbnail Sketch We know that Duncan was youngish, he may have been "Gracious" and "Wise", but there is nothing to suggest that he was outstandingly successful.

THE REIGN

With the accession of Duncan I we might be tempted to think that we are treading familiar ground. We know something of what Swinburne called "the abrupt and steep simplicity of Shakespeare's *Macbeth*". We have in our mind's eye a picture of "the gracious Duncan", old enough to remind Lady Macbeth of her father. We remember how the prophecy of "the weird sisters, hand in hand" stirred the ambition of "black Macbeth" and led to the horror of the King's "most sacrilegious murder". As theatre this is all magnificent; as history it is unreliable.

The work of reference upon which Shakespeare largely drew for this Scottish piece – completed about 1606 in honour of James VI and I – was *The Chronicles of England, Scotland and Ireland* by Raphael Holinshed (1587). Holinshed, in his turn, had made free use of the *History of Scotland* compiled by the celebrated scholar and native of Dundee Hector Boece (*c.* 1465–1536). This distinguished academic, who became Principal of the newly founded King's College, Aberdeen, in 1500 (D.D. of that institution and B.D. of Paris) was a writer whose judgment suffered from the workings of an extremely powerful imagination. As a result Holinshed's account of Duncan, "soft and gentle of nature", of "one Makbeth – somewhat cruell", of "Banquho" – a mythical figure from whom the Stewarts would later claim descent – of

three women "in strange and weird apparell" cannot be regarded
as anything approaching a reliable historical source.

First, then, let it be remembered that in early eleventh-century
Scotland inheritance was not normally determined by what
Gibbon called "the insolent prerogative of primogeniture". The
succession was customarily regulated by the law of tanistry
which meant that the crown, or chieftainship, passed to the person
within the *derbfine* (four generations of kinsmen through male
descent) deemed most suitable on grounds of mental and physical
fitness to rule. Such a system led to frequent and bloody dispute, to
obviate which the reigning monarch often selected a successor, a
king-designate, in his own lifetime. As well as doing this Malcolm
II had liquidated certain individuals who might have competed
for the throne which he destined to his grandson Duncan – but
there were, nevertheless, two kinsfolk of royal blood whose claims
and, no doubt, ambitions led them to disagree with this choice.
They were a lady called Gruoch and her husband, the Mormaer
(Earl) of Moray, whose name was Macbeth.

Duncan, however, became King of Scotland in the full vigour
of manhood and busied himself with military operations which
included an abortive siege of Durham. He then initiated an
equally unsuccessful attempt to reduce his cousin Thorfinn, Earl
of Caithness, now grown to man's estate, only to suffer defeat in
an obscure engagement at Burghead, on the southern shore of

the Moray Firth. He was
now in Macbeth's country –
and hard pressed. Here was
a situation which no power
politician of the period would
have failed to exploit. The
ambitious and frustrated
Mormaer seized the oppor-
tunity and encompassed the
death of his King, probably
in battle near Elgin, on 14
August 1040.

Round Tower, Abernethy, 6 miles south-east of Perth – built, probably, about the time of Duncan I's birth (see also pages 15 and 29)

(*The Scottish Field*)

Macbeth, by Jacob de Witt (or de Wett). See note on portrait
of Duncan I

MACBETH, 1040–1057

(Son of Findlaech, Mormaer of Moray, and Donada, the daughter of MALCOLM II)

Born about 1005, was about 35 when he ascended the throne and about 52 when he was killed.

Married Gruoch. No issue.

Thumbnail Sketch A power politician and man of his time. Not the villain of Shakespeare's essentially Jacobean play.

THE REIGN

After the death of Duncan, Shakespeare continues with the murder of Banquo, the embarrassing appearances of his ghost, the slaughter of Lady Macduff and her children, Lady Macbeth's madness and the invasion of Scotland by Malcolm, son of Duncan, supported by Macduff. The march of their army under a "leafy screen", each man cutting a bough, appears to fulfil the witches' prophecy about Birnam Wood coming to Dunsinane and ends in Macbeth's death on the field of battle. This concludes what Holinshed calls "the detestable cruelties exercised by the tyrant".

Actually, modern historians tend to give this monarch rather a good press. Words like "ability", "liberality", "equity", "prosperity" and "popularity" are to be found in their accounts of the reign. Nevertheless reliable facts are scarce.

It is clear that Macbeth ruled for seventeen years while Duncan's sons were sent to safety in exile. The elder, Malcolm Canmore, aged about nine, went to Siward, Earl of Northumbria, his mother's cousin, and was carried by him to the court of Edward the Confessor, with its Norman-French culture and continental atmosphere. The younger, Donald Bane, some seven years old, was despatched to the Hebrides, where the influences which he underwent were Gaelic and essentially insular.

The quality of "liberality", mentioned above, may perhaps be exemplified by Macbeth and Gruoch's gift of land to the Culdees of Lochleven – one of the most famous houses of a somewhat amorphous Celtic religious order whose many foundations in Scotland and Ireland were characterized by independence, separatism and, as the eleventh century wore on, a marked absence of discipline. There is, further, the record of a visit to Rome in the year 1050 when Macbeth, "King of the Scots", perhaps wishing to insure his immortal soul, which cannot have been totally unburdened, is said to have "scattered money among the poor like sand".

But trouble was brewing south of the Scottish border. In the year 1054 Siward of Northumbria, with the encouragement of Edward the Confessor and accompanied by Malcolm Canmore, now aged twenty-three, advanced north and defeated Macbeth on 27 July (noted by a chronicler, piously if perhaps irrelevantly, as the Feast Day of the Seven Sleepers of Ephesus). This victory is said to have taken place at Dunsinane, with or without the exercise in camouflage recorded by Holinshed and dramatized by Shakespeare. The King then seems to have withdrawn in a northerly direction to be overthrown and killed on 15 August 1057 at Lumphanan, some twenty-five miles west of Aberdeen, where "Macbeth's Cairn" may be seen to this day.

Let Holinshed, accurate at last, have the final word. "This was the end of Makbeth, after he had reigned seventeen yeeres over the Scotishmen."

David Garrick as Macbeth, by Zoffany
(*By courtesy of the Trustees of the Garrick Club*)

Malcolm III (Canmore) – eighteenth century engraving by
Alexander Bannerman

(Scottish National Portrait Gallery)

MALCOLM III (CANMORE – Great Head) 1058–1093

(Son of DUNCAN I and his wife who was a cousin of Siward, Earl of Northumbria)

Born about 1031, was about 27 when he ascended the throne, and about 62 when he was killed.

Married Ingibjorg, ? widow ? daughter of Thorfinn (see pages 24, 30) had three sons of whom DUNCAN II was on the throne for six months in 1094.
Married Margaret, granddaughter of Edmund Ironside – had eight children including:

> Edmund
> EDGAR
> ALEXANDER I
> DAVID I
> Matilda – married Henry I of England
> Mary – married Eustace, Count of Boulogne

Thumbnail Sketch   A fierce, unlettered soldier who adored his cultivated second wife. When not campaigning he upheld her policies and showed a vicarious appreciation of learning by kissing her manuscripts and adorning them with precious bindings.

THE REIGN

The throne of Scotland could not be safely occupied by Malcolm Canmore until the elimination of Macbeth's stepson, Lulach. The sobriquet "fatuus", which the chroniclers gave him, suggests a retarded young man, but this did not stop the arrogation of the kingship to him by the mormaers of Moray (a hot-bed of separatism until 1134), from whose line he sprang. His "reign", however, was short, for Malcolm did him to death in March 1058.

The undefined southern border offered continual attraction to this dedicated soldier, who invaded England on no less than five occasions between 1061 and 1093. But he never achieved his object of establishing permanent and secure rule over the northern counties, and it would be profitless to unravel the tedious details of his bloody campaigns. Nevertheless his depredations, and occasional support of his brother-in-law Edgar Atheling (grandson of Edmund Ironside and claimant to the English throne), brought him up against the Anglo-Norman monarchy, established in 1066 and already on its way to becoming the most powerful in Europe. William the Conqueror, in order to arrest Malcolm's turbulence and encouragement of rebels, mounted a sophisticated combined operation against him in 1072, and received the Scottish King's homage at Abernethy, six miles south-east of Perth. Subsequent Norman action against Scotland included the building of a "New Castle", on the Tyne, by Robert, eldest son of the Conqueror, in 1080, an invasion by William Rufus culminating in another act of homage in 1091, Rufus' annexation of Carlisle in 1092 and, finally, his summoning of Malcolm to do homage at Gloucester in 1093. This journey, which gave Malcolm the opportunity of laying one of the foundation stones of the new Cathedral at Durham, ended in an angry scene and no doubt stimulated the foray to Alnwick on which Malcolm met his death in the autumn of the same year.

Probably the most important event of the reign had occurred in 1067 when Edgar Atheling, with his two sisters – Margaret and Christina – appeared as refugees from the Norman invasion of England. Malcolm, by then a widower, was captivated by Mar-

garet and married her in 1069–70. This not only encouraged him to do battle against England on behalf of his brother-in-law but also exposed his kingdom to religious and cultural influences of the greatest importance. Margaret was a learned and powerful church woman (she was to be canonized in 1250) and her adoring husband was enthusiastically prepared to enforce the ecclesiastical reforms she introduced: use of the Roman rite, clerical celibacy, the keeping of Lent, the Easter mass, the observance of Sunday, etc. He also supported her numerous charitable

St Margaret's Chapel, Edinburgh Castle

(Reproduced by permission of the Department of the Environment. Crown Copyright)

activities, of which Queensferry, for the transport of pilgrims over the Firth of Forth, remains a memorial, while her orthodoxy was exemplified when she replaced, by a modern structure, the Culdee church at Dunfermline. It is something of a relief to learn that this solemn lady (she is reputed never to have laughed) had a flair for interior decoration, an eye for clothes and that she introduced her husband and his rude court to a comparatively civilized cuisine, enlivened by French wines. She is commemorated appropriately, and movingly, by the tiny chapel which crowns Edinburgh's Castle Rock.

The trend of St Margaret of Scotland's policy was Anglo-Norman and anti-Celtic. She had started the process, unwelcome in the northern part of her kingdom, but popular in the South, whereby "the Norman Conquest of Scotland was carried out by the Scottish kings themselves" (Robert L. Mackie. *A Short History of Scotland*).

Donald Bane – eighteenth–nineteenth-century engraving
by Miller

(Scottish National Portrait Gallery)

DONALD BANE, 1093–1097

(Son of DUNCAN I, and his wife, who was a cousin of Siward,
  Earl of Northumbria, brother of MALCOLM CANMORE)

Born about 1033, was about 60 when he ascended the throne and
about 66 when he died.

Married a person unknown – had one daughter:
Bethoc.

Thumbnail Sketch   A rough Celtic reactionary.

THE REIGN

Queen Margaret had been ill for some six months and had,
indeed, received the viaticum, when her son Edgar reached her
bedside in Edinburgh Castle with the news of Malcolm's death.
According to the Anglo-Saxon Chronicle she "prayed of God that
she might give up the ghost", and was rapidly granted her wish.
Donald Bane also reacted with swiftness remarkable for a sexagenarian. He made all speed from his Hebridean exile and had
laid siege to the castle before Margaret's body could be removed
for burial. It was with difficulty that Edgar smuggled it out, in
conditions of fog, that it might be laid to rest in the church which
Margaret had erected at Dunfermline. Thereupon he and his
brothers Alexander and David repaired to England, where their
sisters were already receiving an exacting education at the hands
of their grim aunt Christina, now a nun at Romsey Abbey in
Hampshire. In England the young men came under the protection
of their uncle Edgar Atheling, who had sensibly achieved reconciliation with William Rufus. Malcolm and Margaret's eldest
son, Edmund, alone remained in Scotland, throwing in his lot
with Donald Bane.

Donald Bane represented reaction and found a powerful body
of conservative opinion – particularly among the highlanders of
the North – which offered him support. He and his allies rejected
primogeniture and subscribed to the custom of tanistry (see page
30) on which he now based his claim to the throne. They were,
further, united in disliking the admixture of English blood which

Margaret had transmitted to her children and in detesting the Anglo-Norman religious and cultural innovations which had been generally welcomed in the southern part of the country.

Obviously William Rufus viewed this essentially anti-English turn of events in the North with distaste. In place of the backward-looking Donald Bane he naturally preferred the idea of an anglicized and, if possible, malleable monarch. Such a one was available in the person of the thirty-three-year-old son of Malcolm III and Ingibjorg, Duncan, a hostage in England since the homage at Abernethy. This prince, representing the primogeniture concept ("I Dunecan, son of King Malcolumb, by hereditary right king of Scotia") was accordingly despatched to Scotland with military assistance. He succeeded in seizing and holding the throne as Duncan II for six months of 1094, until Donald Bane and Edmund could contrive his death. Rule was now shared between these two.

But the King of England was persistent in his policy. In 1097 he sponsored another expedition led by Edgar Atheling and accompanied by Edgar, Malcolm and Margaret's second son. Encouraged by a satisfactory vision of St Cuthbert, vouchsafed to young Edgar while in camp near Durham, they advanced confidently. They defeated and deposed Donald Bane, who nevertheless escaped capture until 1099 when he was apprehended. His eyes were put out and he remained a prisoner until death released him in the same year.

Seal of Duncan II in British Museum

(*Mansell Collection*)

Edgar – Seal in British Museum

(*Mansell Collection*)

EDGAR, 1097–1107

(Son of MALCOLM CANMORE and St Margaret, nephew of DONALD BANE)

Born about 1074, was about 23 when he ascended the throne and about 33 when he died.

Unmarried.

Thumbnail Sketch Anglo-Norman in sympathy, a patron of the church, his treatment of Donald Bane suggests a less amiable character than that presented by the monkish chroniclers.

THE REIGN

There now followed, one after another upon the Scottish throne, three sons of Malcolm Canmore and Margaret. All had English blood in their veins, all were English-educated – perhaps having shared the rigours of Romsey with their sisters. But before these southern influences could make themselves felt, dramatic events occurred in the West.

It will be recalled that, in the ninth century, the Norsemen had established themselves in Shetland, Orkney, the Hebrides, Sutherland and Caithness. Early in Edgar's reign certain of these territories were in a state of revolt – thus calling down upon themselves a powerful visitation by Magnus Barelegs, King of Norway from 1093 to 1103–4. He raged through Orkney and the Western Isles – killing, plundering and burning – until, in 1098, he and Edgar made a formal agreement. It was laid down by treaty that all islands west of a line which could be traversed by a vessel with helm in position should be ceded to Norway. It was simple to sail east of Skye, through the Sound of Mull, into Loch Linnhe and round Lismore, through the Firth of Lorne and the Sound of Jura – but Magnus ingeniously added Kintyre to his gains by causing his men to drag his ship overland from Loch Tarbert to Loch Fyne before continuing more conventionally by way of the Kyles of Bute into the Firth of Clyde. And so the area remained in Norwegian hands (though not without disturbances) until the battle of Largs in 1263.

And now there continued that "Norman Conquest of Scotland", to which reference has already been made (see page 39). Edgar owed a debt of gratitude to William Rufus, and this encouraged in him a tendency to look south, exemplified by the beginning of a shift of power from Dunfermline to Edinburgh. But though kings were now likely to sit less frequently ". . . in Dunfermline toun drinking the blude red wine" nevertheless that town's great church became their burial place because Iona now belonged to Magnus Barelegs, just as, for the same reason, coronations were henceforth performed at Scone.

If the King looked south, so ambitious ecclesiastics and military men, greedy for preferment and land, began increasingly to look north, resulting in an advance of Anglo-Norman culture, and the administrative ideas expressed by feudalism, through the Southern Uplands and Central Lowlands, but not penetrating what was virtually *terra incognita* beyond the Highland line. Links with a more sophisticated world were further strengthened by dynastic marriages. In 1100 Edgar's sister Matilda was wedded to Henry I of England. She was to become the mother of William, who went down in the White Ship, and of another Matilda who, having married Henry V, the Holy Roman (Germanic) Emperor, married again, after his death, Geoffrey of Anjou and returned to her native land to compete for its throne against Stephen (1135–1154). In 1102 Edgar's second sister Mary became the wife of

Eustace of Boulogne and added yet another member to this bewildering series of Matildas in the person of a daughter who became Stephen's Queen. As a pendant to these foreign relations it is agreeable to record that in 1105 Edgar favoured the Irish king Murchertach with the rare, if mildly incongruous, gift of a camel.

The Guthrie Bell Shrine (the figure of Christ crucified
dates from about 1100)

(National Museum of Antiquities of Scotland)

In 1107 Edgar, by then benefactor of Saint Andrews, Dunfermline, Coldingham and Durham, died in the odour of sanctity,
to receive later a most flattering write-up by the monastic
chronicler Ailred of Rievaulx.

A SILVER COIN
AND

THE GREAT SEAL OF ALEXANDER I.

Alexander I – Great Seal

(*Mansell Collection*)

ALEXANDER I, 1107–1124

(Son of MALCOLM CANMORE and St Margaret; brother of EDGAR)

Born about 1077, was about 31 when he ascended the throne and about 48 when he died.

Married Sibylla, natural daughter of Henry I of England. No issue by her.
Had an illegitimate son: Malcolm.

Thumbnail Sketch A man of learning and religion, who ruled his people with severity and supported the church with generosity.

THE REIGN

Though Alexander I now succeeded Edgar, the latter, by what seems a peculiar stroke of policy, had bequeathed Strathclyde, Cumbria and a part of Lothian to his younger brother David. This meant that David, as the virtually independent Earl of Cumbria, ruled the West (apart from the territory ceded to Magnus Barelegs) from the Solway to the Clyde. Alexander, though unenthusiastic about these arrangements, had to acquiesce, owing to the Anglo-Norman support which David enjoyed. He himself governed the eastern part of the country, his authority weakening with every northward step and petering out into a loose suzerainty once the Spey was passed. Nevertheless this King was reputedly "ane gritt punisher of malefactours and evil doars", as the turbulent inhabitants of Moray (supported by those of Mearns) learned to their cost when they descended upon him at Invergowrie in yet another outburst of Celtic resentment at the process of Europeanization, emanating from England, which had been started by St Margaret and was continued during the reigns of her sons.

Alexander had strengthened his ties with the South by marrying Sibylla, a natural daughter of his brother-in-law Henry I. This lovely and civilized lady brought with her some of the customs and comforts of the more sophisticated court which had been her home, and a new sumptuousness is perhaps detectable when we read of the King's gift to St Andrews Cathedral of "his comely steed of Araby" decked out with "many a precious fair jewel".

Patronage of the Church, the standard-bearer *par excellence* of contemporary European civilization, was an essential part of Alexander's ruling technique (every bit as important as the introduction of the great administrative offices of Chancellor and Constable – titles which we hear for the first time in this reign). He was a benefactor of St Andrews and Dunfermline and initiated proper diocesan organization by reviving the see of Dunkeld and founding that of Moray. Scone Priory was established in 1120 and its inmates were given responsibility for a chapel on the Island of Women in Loch Tay, which the King caused to be built in memory of Sibylla, who died in 1122. An abbey rose on the island of Inchcolm in the Firth of Forth – an expression of thanksgiving for Alexander's preservation in a storm – and all these institutions were placed in the hands of the Augustinian Canons (also known as Austin Canons and Canons Regular), who may be regarded as Alexander's spearhead of European Catholic Orthodoxy, directed against the old Celtic Christianity.

In this connection it is significant that Robert, Prior of Scone, was elected Bishop of St Andrews in 1124, an appointment which ended a long period of disputes about the consecration of bishops

to that see. First Alexander had chosen Turgot, the Prior of Durham who had been his mother's confessor, but Turgot upheld the claims of York to Scotland's obedience. Similarly his successor Eadmer supported the pretensions of Canterbury, where he had hitherto worked as precentor and historian. Both these were forced to return home, for though Alexander required the professionalism of southern churchmen, he could not accept any theory which might prejudice his own inde-

Inchcolm Abbey and the Central Isthmus (Firth of Forth)
(By courtesy of Mr Campbell R. Steven)

pendence or that of his kingdom. Eventually his object was achieved for, when Robert was consecrated in 1128, the Archbishop of York accepted a carefully worded escape clause which made clear that no obedience was enforceable or admissible. But this success was posthumous. Alexander had died at Stirling four years previously.

David I and his grandson Malcolm IV (Charter of Kelso Abbey, 1159)

(National Library of Scotland. By kind permission of the Duke of Roxburghe)

DAVID I, 1124–1153

(Son of MALCOLM CANMORE and St Margaret, brother of EDGAR and ALEXANDER I)

Born about 1080, was about 44 when he ascended the throne and about 73 when he died.

Married Matilda of Huntingdon – had four children including:
> Henry, Earl of Northumberland and Huntingdon (died 1152)

Thumbnail Sketch Civilized, pious, accessible, a great patron of the church and a feudal monarch in the Anglo-Norman tradition, David I was in the nature of a Scottish St Louis.

THE REIGN

David, like Edgar and Alexander, had received an English education and had experienced life at the court of his brother-in-law Henry I (Beauclerc). William of Malmesbury writes, not without a hint of patronage: "his manners were thus polished from the rust of Scottish barbarity" and certainly he was more Normanized than any of his predecessors. Marriage brought him English riches and English titles (the lordships of Northampton and Huntingdon), and thus provided the opportunity, invaluable to one who had already seen central government functioning, of observing Norman administration at the local level. The Earldom of Cumbria (see page 49) then provided a practical testing ground, and, as feudal order advanced, as an abbey rose at Selkirk (1113 – later moved to Kelso) and a priory at Jedburgh (1118) "coming events cast their shadows before".

It was thus a formidable monarch against whom the traditionally factious men of Moray rebelled, yet again, in 1130. But David had subdued them by 1134 when, characteristically, he parcelled out their land among his Norman adherents.

And there were external problems as well. In 1135 Henry I of England died. The situation whereby his daughter Matilda, David's niece, entered upon a struggle for the throne with her cousin Stephen is familiar. Matilda enjoyed David's support, for, like his father, he had an eye on England's northern counties. In fact he made four expeditions into England on Matilda's behalf, of which the best-known occurred in 1138 when the ferocious gallantry and tactical ineptitude of his Galloway contingent lost him the Battle of the Standard near Northallerton. But military failure can be offset by diplomatic success and, in 1139, David achieved the Earldom of Northumberland for his son Henry.

Before, during and after what may be called the "Stephen-Matilda period" David, a firm believer in the alliance of throne and altar, was busy with the foundation and patronage of religious houses, mostly manned by two powerful eleventh-century orders – the Augustinian Canons and the Cistercians, before whose orthodoxy and competence the anachronistic Culdees were forced into slow withdrawal. These institutions, nine in all,* occasioned considerable financial outlay and later caused James I to observe ruefully that his pious predecessor had been "a sore saint for the crown" – but they represent a vital factor in the advance of civilization and order. Ecclesiastical and governmental

RUINS OF MELROSE ABBEY

efficiency was further promoted by the addition of six dioceses to the three † already in existence, within which parishes began to be formed.

Closely linked with these church developments was the spread in Scotland of feudalism on the English pattern – based on landholding in return for service – the form of society familiar to David's French-speaking Anglo-Norman followers, who now saw their hopes of new wealth and power fulfilled. Foreign names appeared, which Scotland would make her own:

* Cambuskenneth, Dryburgh, Dundrennan, Holyrood, Jedburgh, Kelso, Kinloss, Melrose, Newbattle.

† Already in existence: Dunkeld, Moray, St Andrews. Added: Aberdeen, Brechin, Caithness, Dunblane, Glasgow, Ross.

Silver Coin of David I

(*National Museum of Antiquities of Scotland*)

Bailleul (Balliol), de Brus (Bruce), and there was also a nobleman of Breton extraction whom David made Steward of his kingdom, a title from which, eventually, "Stewart" was to be derived. At the same time these innovations actually stimulated and consolidated the indigenous clan system, whereby men were held together by the blood relationship with their chief; for the advance of Europeanization, developing steadily in the Lowlands, stopped short of the Highlands in the North and West, where Gaelic-speaking Celts lived and fought traditionally until disaster overtook Prince Charles Edward in 1746.

And so, with his bastions of monasteries, cathedrals, feudal castles and royal burghs (towns bound to the King by charters which conferred land, trade facilities, rights of self-government, monopolies, etc. in return for service or cash) David imposed upon Scotland an order hitherto unknown and a prosperity previously unfamiliar. A great work was in being when, in May 1153, the King died at Carlisle "in an attitude of devotion".

Malcolm IV – Seal

(*Mansell Collection*)

MALCOLM IV (THE MAIDEN), 1153–1165

(Son of Henry, Earl of Northumberland and Huntingdon –
see page 53 – and Ada de Warenne. Grandson of DAVID I)

Born 1141–2, was 11 when he ascended the throne and 23 when
he died.

Unmarried.

Thumbnail Sketch This young King, whose nickname refers to
virginity rather than effeminacy, made a not unsuccessful attempt
to govern in the tradition of his grandfather.

THE REIGN

The death, in June 1152, of David I's only son Henry, Earl of
Northumberland, might well have proved a dynastic disaster.
The fact that this was not the case is evidence of the considerable
power which the monarchy had by now acquired, and represents
the first clear victory for primogeniture.

The Earl left three sons: Malcolm, William and David. The
first two became Kings of Scotland, the third fathered three
daughters whose progeny featured in the dispute for the crown of
1290.

The immediate problem, in 1152, was to make certain that
Malcolm should succeed his grandfather. David achieved this by
sending the child on a progress with the Earl of Fife, during which
he was proclaimed heir and generally accepted – his coronation
at Scone followed in due course.

Malcolm, then, inherited a Scotland which, outside the Highland line and despite sporadic upheavals, was assuming an
Anglo-Norman as opposed to a Celtic character. The great Catholic church, the feudal system of landholding, the burghs, the
officials of the Royal Household (the Justiciar, Chancellor, Cham-
berlain, Marshal, Constable, etc.), the Sheriffs operating from
royal castles at the local level (though there were as yet no shires) –
all this derives its inspiration from the England of Henry I which
was itself European.

Nevertheless the accession of an eleven-year-old king invited trouble. Somerled, a powerful Celtic-Norse chieftain based on Argyll, having made himself independent of the successors to Magnus Barelegs, ruled significant tracts of western Scotland with a number of the adjacent islands – an area virtually equivalent to seventh-century Dalriada (see page 18). It was a delight to this fierce "Lord of the Isles" to march east in search of plunder and to the discomfiture of the Anglo-Normans – so he remained an intermittent menace until he met his death in battle at Renfrew in 1164. And there were other uprisings, notably in Moray and Galloway, which were also eventually crushed.

Here was a measure of success, but relations with England presented a more difficult problem. David I had been able to fish in the troubled waters of the Stephen-Matilda sea and had, as a result, established himself in Cumberland, Westmorland and Northumberland. His possession of these counties had been expressly confirmed by Henry Plantagenet in 1149 when he came, cap in hand, to beg assistance for his mother, Matilda. But Henry Plantagenet was now the dynamic Henry II of England and quite prepared, like other politicians down the ages, to act on the dictum of William Rufus: "Who is there that can fulfil all that he promises?" He was well enough established in 1157 to summon Malcolm to Chester, there to divest him of the three coveted northern counties, allowing, in return, the restoration of the previously confiscated Earldom of Huntingdon. Some sort of homage was probably made by Malcolm in 1158 or 1159, after

which he accompanied Henry on an expedition to Toulouse, receiving the honour of knighthood at his hands at Tours. These Anglo-Scottish transactions did not arouse the enthusiasm of Malcolm's subjects and gave rise to some of the disturbances to which reference has been made.

Nevertheless when Malcolm died at Jedburgh, in December 1165, it was not without achievements. He had, indeed, reigned creditably in the tradition of his grandfather. Rebels had been sub-

RUINS OF KELSO ABBEY

Nave of Dunfermline Abbey *c.* 1150

(By courtesy of Mr G. Allan Little)

dued, feudalization continued, and it appears that the daily business of government was competently discharged by the Household. Indeed the meticulous and increasingly sophisticated paper work performed by that body was, in itself, a step towards uniformity and the consolidation of the realm.

William I – Great Seal

(*Mansell Collection*)

WILLIAM I (THE LION), 1165–1214

(Son of Henry, Earl of Northumberland and Huntingdon – see page 53 – and Ada de Warenne. Brother of MALCOLM IV)

Born 1143, was 22 when he ascended the throne and 71 when he died.

Married Ermengarde de Bellomonte – had four children:
    ALEXANDER II
    and three daughters who married into England

Thumbnail Sketch   Another monarch in the tradition of David I. Probably called "The Lion" from his interest in the advance of law – "*leo justitiae*" – rather than from any outstanding qualities of strength or courage.

THE REIGN

William ascended the throne with his eye firmly fixed on the counties of Cumberland, Westmorland and Northumberland, which Henry II of England had recovered from Malcolm IV in 1157. He took the opportunity of a Royal expedition to Normandy in 1166 to suggest their return (as Earl of Huntingdon he was accompanying the great Plantagenet). This provoked one of the violent scenes which were a commonplace with Henry II, and led William to make overtures to Louis VII of France. In this we may detect the inception of the Franco-Scottish friendship later to be romanticized in the words "The Auld Alliance".

However, a more favourable opportunity was soon to present itself. Henry II faced many difficulties in the years immediately following the murder of Thomas à Becket (December 1170) – not least the treasonable activities of his sons, urged on by their formidable mother, Eleanor of Aquitaine. William, allied with these royal rebels, descended confidently upon Alnwick in 1174. With his forces dispersed and his security unheeded he was captured while disporting himself in knightly fashion and carried off to Henry with all the indignities then deemed suitable for such an occasion.

Henry, smarting after the famous penance for his share in the martyrdom of a saint (Becket had been canonized in 1173), was in no lenient mood. Previous Scottish monarchs had made vague acts of homage to his predecessors – there was nothing vague about what happened now. By the Treaty of Falaise (December 1174) William became, beyond all argument or doubt, Henry's feudal vassal, the Church in Scotland was declared subordinate to the Church in England, and the castles of Stirling, Edinburgh, Roxburgh and Jedburgh were occupied by English troops.

The situation looked unpromising but, during the fifteen years which elapsed before this burden was lifted, various rays of light enlivened the potential gloom. The Church in Scotland contrived to maintain her independence of England, owing to the rivalry which prevented effective co-operation between the English arch-bishops. A long struggle with a number of Popes about the appoint-ment of an incumbent to the see of St Andrews ended, at last, in compromise and, in 1188, Clement III clarified Scotland's ecclesi-astical position by declaring that she came directly under Rome. Nor was an element of malicious humour lacking – in 1178 William founded the priory, later abbey, of Arbroath and, doubtless to exacerbate Henry II, dedicated it to St Thomas of Canterbury.

The summer of 1189 brought important news. Henry died at Chinon and was succeeded by his son Richard Coeur de Lion, who had no thought but for the crusade. For this enterprise cash was needed and 10,000 marks from Scotland purchased the abrogation of the Treaty of Falaise and with it a happy return to the agreeable vagueness of the *status quo ante* – a situation which remained unchanged for the rest of the reign, despite certain mo-ments of tension between William and England's King John during the period 1199 to 1214.

At home, sporadic Celt and Norse rebellions continued in Ross, Caithness, Moray and Gallo-way. They were all, temporarily, suppressed. The policy of estab-lishing burghs continued apace, with consequent profits from

STIRLING CASTLE

Chessmen from Uig, Lewis
(*National Museum of Antiquities of Scotland*)

increased trade, and the beginnings of a civic and political self-consciousness. But the varying fortunes of a long reign had left the monarch old and exhausted. William the Lion died at Stirling in December 1214.

THE GOLDEN AGE
1214–1286

Alexander II	1214–1249
Alexander III	1249–1286

In England		*In France*	
John		Philip II (Augustus)	1180–1223
(Lackland)	1199–1216	Louis VIII	1223–1226
Henry III	1216–1272	Louis IX (St Louis)	1226–1270
Edward I	1272–1307	Philip III (The Bold)	1270–1285
		Philip IV (The Fair)	1285–1314

Pluscarden Abbey, Elgin

(By permission of the Father Abbot)

THE GOLDEN AGE

1214–1286

Scotland did not stand apart from the great European "age of faith", associated with the names of St Dominic (1170–1221) and St Francis of Assisi (1182–1226). Alexander II not only welcomed Dominican and Franciscan friars, but also architectural technicians from foreign parts.

During the thirteenth century in Europe St Louis went on a crusade, the Teutonic Knights carried the Cross into heathen Prussia, St Thomas Aquinas spelt out the official doctrine of the Roman Catholic Church, Dante met Beatrice and Gothic art attained its climax.

In Scotland, enjoying a brief "Golden Age", we find the "Gothic Pointed Style" or "First Pointed Gothic" (known to some of us, previously, as "Early English"). There rose a number of cathedrals, abbeys and parish churches of distinction among which Glasgow, Elgin and the Abbey of Pluscarden (near Elgin) – now re-roofed and inhabited by a flourishing Benedictine community – may, perhaps, make a special appeal.

Kings and magnates could afford to build in stone, and did so not only for the greater glory of God; which means that there are plenty of sophisticated castles to visit. Dunstaffnage, near Oban, stands as a memorial to Alexander II's ambition to drive the Norsemen from the Hebrides; Rothesay was brought up to date during this century and Kildrummy (on A97, some 15 miles south of Huntly) was established by Gilbert of Moravia, Bishop of Caithness, as a *point d'appui* from which to dominate the Highland frontier.

Alexander II – Great Seal

(*Mansell Collection*)

ALEXANDER II, 1214–1249

(Son of WILLIAM THE LION and Ermengarde de Bellomonte)

Born 1198, was 16 when he ascended the throne and 50 when he died.

Married Joan, daughter of John of England. No issue.
Married Marie de Couci – had one son:

ALEXANDER III

Thumbnail Sketch   A strong churchman, ruthless politician and strict ruler. Matthew Paris describes him as "justly beloved by all the English as well as his own people".

THE REIGN

Few reigns have passed, as yet, without a disturbance created by the men of Moray. On the present occasion these northern Celtic malcontents were up in arms at once, but met defeat at the hands of a brother Celt – one Makintagart, later to become Earl of Ross - who, after his victory, made a grisly demonstration of loyalty by presenting his King with a number of severed heads. The day of Makintagart's success was 15 June 1215 – the very one upon which John of England was meeting his barons at Runnymede and putting his seal to the Great Charter, a dispute which had already aroused Alexander's lively interest.

For it seemed to Alexander, as it had seemed to certain of his predecessors, that any embarrassment suffered by the English monarchy meant an opportunity to secure Cumberland, Westmorland and Northumberland. For this reason he allied himself with John's opponents, only to suffer discomfiture when the former, encouraged by Innocent III's annulment of Magna Carta, pushed north with an army of mercenaries hoping, as Matthew Paris wrote, "to smoke the little red fox out of his covert". Flames flickered over Berwick, Roxburgh, Coldingham, Dunbar and Haddington. Alexander retaliated by invading England and putting his services at the disposal of the French Dauphin (later Louis VIII) who was aiding the insurgents. But John died in

October 1216 and was succeeded by the nine-year-old Henry III; Louis was defeated in 1217 and withdrew to France; Magna Carta was confirmed and reconciliation achieved between the Kings of England and Scotland. Despite certain moments of tension this reconciliation lasted throughout the reign. Alexander cut his losses over the northern counties, contenting himself with certain small estates for which he was prepared to do homage to Henry. He married Henry's sister Joan, and his own sisters contracted alliances with English notables. The *rapprochement* was finalized by the Treaty of York (1237) and, when a crisis arose some seven years later, good sense prevailed and agreement was restored by the Treaty of Newcastle of 1244.

Alexander's main preoccupation at home was with the enforcement of the rule of law. Certain persons in Caithness became indignant over the alleged rapacity with which Adam, their bishop, levied the tithe. They expressed their feelings by treating this ecclesiastic to various types of assault and battery, and administered a barbarous *coup de grâce* by burning his kitchen over his head. The King had their hands and feet removed and exacted compensation from the local Earl, who had either been indifferent to or in collusion with the criminals. On the other hand one may set against this severity the fact that Alexander was alive to the absurdity of trial by ordeal, and to the disadvantages suffered by women and priests in trial by battle. Both these matters attracted his reforming attention. But insurrection was ruthlessly suppressed, as certain rebels in Argyll (1222), Moray (1225) and Galloway

(1235 and 1248) learnt to their cost. Indeed it was on a punitive expedition that Alexander died. He had long planned to recover the Hebrides for the Scottish crown and, when negotiations with King Haakon IV of Norway proved fruitless, decided on military action, based on the *point d'appui* of Dunstaffnage Castle. But first he must subdue the Macdougalls of Lorne. He did not get far – attacked by fever he died on the Island of Kerrera in the bay of Oban on

The Church of St Athernase, Leuchars (Fife). This twelfth-century Romanesque church – tower later – was consecrated in 1244 (*The Scottish Field*)

8 July 1249.

Alexander was buried, as he had wished, at the Cistercian house of Melrose. He himself had founded two abbeys – Balmerino and Pluscarden – but the modernity of his churchmanship is demonstrated by his patronage of the newly founded orders of friars – the Franciscans (1209) and Dominicans (1220). This meant that Scotland was not left out of the great religious revival which characterized the thirteenth century.

Detail from 'Parliament of Edward I' in 1274,
showing Alexander III sitting on the King's right

(By courtesy of the Trustees of the British Museum)

ALEXANDER III, 1249–1286
(Son of ALEXANDER II and Marie de Couci)

Born 1241, was 7 when he ascended the throne and 44 when he died.

Married Margaret, daughter of Henry III of England – had three children:

>Margaret – married Eric II of Norway, died 1283
>Alexander – died 1283
>David – died 1281

Married Yolande of Dreux. No issue.

Thumbnail Sketch   An effective ruler of strong character whose death left Scotland "stad . . . in perplexity".

THE REIGN

The principle of primogeniture was now firmly enough accepted for there to be no objection to the consecration of this small boy at Scone, a ceremony at which a Celtic bard obliged with a recitation of the young King's genealogy in Gaelic. A year later the balance between ancient and modern traditions was maintained by the translation of St Margaret's body to a sumptuous shrine, the remains of which may still be viewed in the present parish church of Dunfermline. A period of regencies followed with, inevitably, tedious rivalries between those thought to represent a national ideal and others accused of anglophile tendencies. The institution of kingship was, however, strong enough to survive these stresses until Alexander assumed power personally in 1262.

His first preoccupation was with the Hebrides, which his father had hoped to recover from Norway. But Haakon IV was still uninterested in negotiation and had no intention of surrendering the islands. When attacked by the Earl of Ross the Hebridean chiefs called on "Old Haakon" for aid and he left Bergen (he was 59) with a considerable fleet in July 1263. He anchored, menacingly, off Arran, while Alexander, with an eye to the equinoctial gales, resorted to delaying tactics. Dominican friars scuttled to and fro between the monarchs – using every artifice to keep the enemy inactive. At the end of September the longed-for storm blew up and a number of Norwegian ships, sheltering by the Cumbraes, were driven ashore on "the glorious plain" of Largs. A party was landed to cover their withdrawal and, after a muddled minor action, a number put off and sailed for home. Haakon died at Kirkwall, in Orkney – fortified by readings from the sagas – as the year drew to its close. By the Treaty of Perth (1266) the Isle of Man and the Hebrides came to Alexander, for the sum of 4,000 marks and an additional 100 marks per year, and, though Orkney and Shetland were not acquired until 1469, the Norse threat was over. This fact was recognized in 1281 by the marriage of Norway's King Eric II with Alexander's daughter Margaret.

There followed a period of twenty-three years, generally celebrated as a Golden Age. Scotland, with a population which has been estimated at some 400,000 souls, enjoyed external peace and the burgeoning of national self-consciousness. Agriculture was on the up-grade, sheep farming was on the increase, there were fish, furs, skins and wool to export, while those who could afford such luxuries enjoyed imported cloth, corn, spices and wine. Many burghs, in which foreign tongues – particularly that of the Flemings – could be heard, prospered. Stone castles, together with abbeys and cathedrals of greatly increased architectural sophistication, arose, and seekers after learning left their native heath for the universities of England and the continent. It was a time of promise, but one when chance intervened in history.

RUINS OF ELGIN CATHEDRAL

Lead Plate (*c.* 1250) from Kirkwall – the inscription, expanded, reads: "HIC REQUIESCIT WILELMUS SENEX FELICIS MEMORIE PRIMUS EPISCOPUS"
(*National Museum of Antiquities of Scotland*)

The years 1275 to 1286 saw a series of tragedies. First Margaret, Alexander's Queen – sister of Edward I of England – died. Her death was followed, during the years 1281–1283, by those of all her children. In 1285, hoping to re-establish the succession, Alexander married Yolande of Dreux. But a tradition grew up that a ghostly harbinger of death had attended these nuptials at Jedburgh. For, in 1286, on a stormy March night, when riding to join his bride at Kinghorn on the northern shore of the Firth of Forth, Alexander's horse stumbled over a cliff near Pettycur Bay and threw him fatally. "Scotland mournyd him full sare" and the inscription on a roadside monument, erected six hundred years later, reads:

"To the illustrious Alexander III
the last of Scotland's Celtic Kings,
who was accidentally killed near this spot."

THE STRUGGLE FOR
INDEPENDENCE
1286–1406

Margaret (The Maid of Norway)	1286–1290
John Balliol	1292–1296
Interregnum	1296–1306
Robert I (The Bruce)	1306–1329
David II	1329–1371
Robert II (Stewart)	1371–1390
Robert III	1390–1406

In England		*In France*	
Edward I	1272–1307	Philip IV (The Fair)	1285–1314
Edward II	1307–1327	Louis X	
Edward III	1327–1377	(The Quarrelsome)	1314–1316
Richard II	1377–1399	John I	1316
Henry IV	1399–1413	Philip V (The Tall)	1316–1322
		Charles IV (The Fair)	1322–1328
		Philip VI	1328–1350
		John II (The Good)	1350–1364
		Charles V (The Wise)	1364–1380
		Charles VI	1380–1422

Tantallon Castle and the Bass Rock (near North Berwick)

(*The Scottish Field*)

THE STRUGGLE FOR INDEPENDENCE

1286–1406

The memorials to the two great heroes of this time – Sir William Wallace and Robert the Bruce – do not, of course, date from the period. You will, however, no doubt keep your eyes open for them at Paisley, at Abbey Craig near Stirling, at Dunfermline, at Aberdeen and – presented in audio-visual form by the National Trust for Scotland – at Bannockburn. (By which token it would not be irrelevant to visit also, at Burgh-by-Sands, 6 miles north-west of Carlisle, the monument to Edward I of England, "the Hammer of the Scots".)

Troubled days do not encourage ecclesiastical building, but it is well to recollect that Sweetheart Abbey, near Dumfries, started in 1273, was under construction during the fourteenth century. Similarly Dunkeld Cathedral dates from 1318 and work was still in progress upon it almost one hundred years later. There is some admirable decorated Gothic at Melrose and, though Aberdeen's Brig o' Balgownie can hardly be classified as a sacred edifice it was, at least, the work of a fourteenth-century bishop.

These years, characteristically, produced a fine crop of castles. Dunnottar, near Stonehaven; Doune, on the road from Stirling to Callander; and Bothwell, within easy reach of Glasgow, are three among many. And when you are at North Berwick abandon your golf clubs for a spell in order to see Dirleton and Tantallon:

> "Broad, massive, high and stretching far,
> And held impregnable in war."

Official seal for the guardians of Scotland after the death
of Alexander III. Used 1286–1292

Mansell Collection)

MARGARET (THE MAID OF NORWAY), 1286–1290

(Daughter of Eric II of Norway and Margaret, daughter of ALEXANDER III. Granddaughter of ALEXANDER III)

Born ? 1283, was about 3 when she succeeded and about 8 when she died.

Unmarried.

Thumbnail Sketch "So long a poor unknown" (*Cymbeline*, Act IV, Scene 4).

THE REIGN

The three children of Alexander III had died before their father (see pages 73, 75). Therefore in 1284 – after these catastrophes – the King and notables in conference at Scone designated his granddaughter, Margaret, "The Maid of Norway", as heiress. Once again the principle of primogeniture had been accepted and it survived the crisis of 1286. On Alexander's death the infant Princess was declared Queen, and six guardians were chosen to carry on the government until such time as she could shoulder this burden herself.

The arrangement was highly acceptable to Margaret's father, Eric II of Norway, who looked forward to the day when the ill-fortune of Largs would be reversed by the establishment of his daughter upon the Scottish throne. Meanwhile he was not free from immediate anxieties, for there were others, notably Robert Bruce, Earl of Annandale (grandfather of the national hero), who fancied their claims and might well attempt to help themselves to the Maid's heritage before she was in a position to enjoy it. So Eric consulted Edward I of England and negotiations between Norwegians, Scots and English started at Salisbury in 1289, culminating in the Treaty of Birgham (some sixteen miles south-west of Berwick), in 1290. It was here laid down that Margaret should marry Edward of Carnarvon, later Edward II – an immensely sensible solution to a number of problems and one which was agreed without prejudice to the independence of the northern kingdom.

Edward I now sent a fine ship to bring the little Queen across the North Sea. Victualled with abundant meat, and stimulants suitable for adult passengers, her stores also included figs, gingerbread, honey, raisins and sugar to delight the child. But Eric wished his daughter to travel under Norwegian auspices, and so it was in a vessel of her native land that she took passage to Orkney where, in late September 1290, she died.

Sharp competition for the kingship ensued. Thirteen persons put forward claims to the crown and bloodshed seemed imminent. To avert this the Bishop of St Andrews approached Edward I, who, with a statesmanlike eye to the main chance, was more than prepared to act as umpire in the debate.

It was soon clear that there were only three serious candidates: John Balliol the grandson of Margaret, eldest daughter of David, Earl of Huntingdon – see page 57. (He was, additionally, son of the John Balliol who, because he had "enormously damnified" the churches of Durham and Tynemouth, was condemned to public corporal punishment and forced to become a benefactor of the university of Oxford where presently four students, accommodated in an almshouse, gave a modest start to the great college which bears his name. His widow commemorated him by

SWEETHEART ABBEY

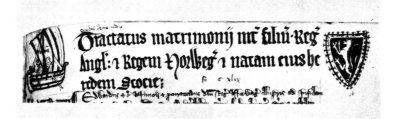

Detail from contemporary copy of document negotiating
marriage treaty between the Maid of Norway and Edward,
son of Edward I of England

founding the Kirkcudbrightshire abbey charmingly called "Sweetheart".) Next was the octogenarian Robert Bruce, Earl of Annan-
dale, son of Isabel, second daughter of David of Huntingdon. He
played a strong card in maintaining that, in 1238, when Alexander
II was still without an heir, he had been named as successor.
Finally came John Hastings, grandson of the third daughter Ada.
Clearly Robert Bruce was the closest relation to Huntingdon, but
Balliol was of the senior line, and it was increasingly believed that
primogeniture was "the ground settled by God for monarchy".
So, after a conference at Norham-on-Tweed in 1291, where the
candidates, in their desire for preferment, acknowledged Edward
I as their feudal superior, there were further deliberations at
Berwick. In late 1292 these culminated in favour of Balliol, and
Edward was able to announce his decision on 17 November. There
followed Balliol's unequivocal act of homage at Norham, his
coronation at Scone and, on the day after Christmas, a confirma-
tory oath of fealty at Newcastle. The clock had been put back one
hundred and eighteen years. John Balliol was as much Edward's
man as if the Treaty of Falaise had never been abrogated.

John Balliol – Great Seal

(*Mansell Collection*)

JOHN BALLIOL, 1292–1296

(Son of John Balliol and his wife Devorguilla of Galloway.
Great-great-great-grandson of DAVID I)

Born about 1250, was about 42 when he ascended the throne,
about 46 when he relinquished it and about 63 when he died.

Married Isabella de Warenne, daughter of John de Warenne,
Earl of Surrey – had two sons:

Edward

Henry

Thumbnail Sketch They called him "Toom Tabard" (empty
surcoat) and he reigned ingloriously.

THE REIGN

The manner of his accession did not commend John Balliol to
all his countrymen, nor had Edward I any intention of loosening
the hold upon the northern kingdom which he had been at pains
to achieve. Exercising the traditional rights of the feudal over-
lord, he lent a ready ear to any who now appealed to him from
Scottish justice, and seized gladly upon the slightest pretext to
summon Scotland's King to his presence – e.g. over the matter of
a bill for wine left unpaid by Alexander III.

In 1294 Philip IV of France, whose relations with England had
been deteriorating for two years past, seized Gascony, which
Edward ruled as Duke of Aquitaine. As part of his mobilization
plans the English monarch called upon Balliol to render him
military and financial assistance – but, even to "Toom Tabard",
this demand seemed excessive. With the support of a council of
twelve notables gathered at Scone in July 1295 he declined to
obey the order, ejected Englishmen from their Scottish estates and
entered into negotiations with France ("The Auld Alliance"
again – see page 61).

These measures, and a not very effective Scottish incursion
into Northumberland and Cumberland, aroused the formidable
anger of "fell Edward". He advanced upon Berwick, where a
particularly loathsome sack and slaughter ensued in March 1296.

In the next month John de Warenne, Earl of Surrey, was victorious at Dunbar, and, except for a seven- to ten-day resistance by Edinburgh Castle, what followed was a conqueror's *promenade militaire*.

A series of humiliations were now inflicted upon Balliol and his country. With degrading ceremonial at the church of Strachathro, four miles north-east of Brechin, on 7 July, and with further abasement at Brechin three days later, he repudiated the French treaty and gave up his kingdom. Thereafter the wretched man departed to imprisonment in England, from which he was released after three years, to die at his French castle of Hélicourt in 1313.

Edward concluded his easy campaign by an advance to Elgin. He then visited Scone and possessed himself of the Stone of Destiny, to be placed beneath England's Coronation Chair. It was, naturally, rumoured that the ingenious canons who were its guardians had hidden the original on the historic hill of Dunsinane and fobbed off the victor with a substitute. Were this the case, the elaborately planned and successfully executed escapade of 1950–1951, when the stone vanished from the abbey of Westminster and reappeared in that of Arbroath, would seem to fall a trifle flat. To this acquisition Edward added the crown of the Scottish Kings, St Margaret's piece of the true cross, and a mass of the defeated country's documentary records.

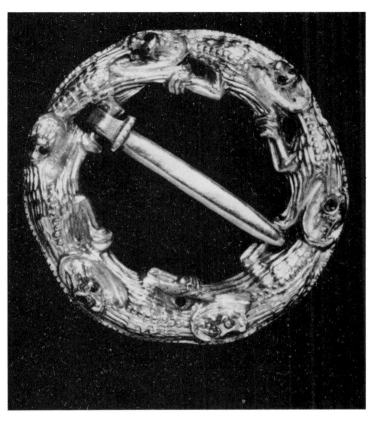

The Kames Brooch (*c.* 1300)
(*National Museum of Antiquities of Scotland*)

The last scene in this particular act of the Edwardian Anglo-Scottish drama took place at Berwick. Many Scots had supported the English King (Balliol had not stimulated general loyalty, and frequently there was the question of the feudal obligations incurred by those who possessed estates in England). As a result some two thousand of them gathered – a great many of their names can be read to this day in the so-called "Ragman Rolls" – Edward was pleased to accept their allegiance and then, with rude words about *ordure* (filth), he left thankfully for the South.

Sir William Wallace – Bronze Statue by W. Grant Stevenson,
at Aberdeen

(Photograph by Aberdeen Corporation Publicity Department)

INTERREGNUM, 1296–1306

Edward's thankfulness at leaving Scotland may well have been combined with ill-founded confidence – for he was soon campaigning in Flanders. Meanwhile the great castles commanding Scotland's strategic points were occupied by the English and the government of the country placed in the hands of an English triumvirate: John de Warenne as Guardian, Hugh Cressingham – a clerical figure – as Treasurer, and William Ormsby as Justiciar. The land was troubled and restive.

At this moment there arose a hero, Sir William Wallace. He was probably born at Elderslie by Paisley in about 1270. In May 1297 he killed an English sheriff at Lanark. This deed captured the popular imagination and, at astonishing speed, its perpetrator was joined by malcontents from north, south, east and west. Under him they formed an army, commanded, admittedly, by a knight, but one in which the great nobles of Scotland seldom led or served. Many strongholds fell before it and, after three months, it was besieging Dundee. In September de Warenne and Cressingham advanced to make good the safety of that great fortress where "Stirling, like a huge brooch, clasps Highlands and Lowlands together."* Wallace was there before them, disposed on the slopes of Abbey Craig (now crowned by his great monument, completed in 1869), ready to deny their crossing of the Forth. De Warenne, surprisingly, accepted Cressingham's inexpert tactical advice, and presented the Scots with a situation of which they took swift and ferocious advantage.

After this signal success at Stirling Bridge (11 September 1297) (where Wallace lost his valued second-in-command – Sir Andrew Moray) the fierce victors made a sharp plundering raid into Northumberland and Cumberland and their leader assumed the title of Guardian of Scotland, which he ruled in the name of John Balliol. He proudly informed the Hanse towns of Hamburg and Lübeck that they could trade once more with an independent Scottish kingdom, and awaited the reaction of Edward I. It was not long delayed. In 1298 that determined soldier advanced across the border, and over scorched earth, intent on finding

* Alexander Smith, *A Summer in Skye*.

Wallace's army and destroying it. At last the vital intelligence was received – the enemy lay near Falkirk. The Scots were heavily outnumbered, and although their schiltrons (squares of spearmen) offered long and gallant resistance, they were eventually overcome by the fire-power of archers and the shock of cavalry. This defeat (22 July 1298) rang down the curtain on the Wallace drama. Seven years elapsed before its bloody epilogue.

"The Liberator" now took to the forest and, perhaps, the continent. A dismal cloud settled upon Scotland, with English armies campaigning almost annually against resistance offered mainly by John Comyn of Badenoch, Balliol's nephew. He, however, submitted to Edward in 1304. In the next year Edward achieved his heart's desire. The hiding place of William Wallace was revealed to a certain Sir John Menteith, "fause Menteith", who handed him over to Edward. There followed the famous trial in Westminster Hall and the revolting punishment for treason at Smithfield. As well as placing the victim's head on London Bridge there were other ghastly exhibits at Newcastle, Berwick, Stirling and Perth. In Scotland these gruesome trophies did as much to stir up national spirit as had ever been the case with the lost leader's "banners and gonfanons".

Edward now made a final attempt to solve his northern problem by the "Ordinance for the Government of Scotland", a sensible, even conciliatory settlement, which foundered in the storm of yet another national uprising. The new hero was Robert Bruce, grandson of the claimant of 1291 – now defunct (see pages 81, 83). Young Bruce had, hitherto, been playing a complicated game in which the one constant factor was his burning desire to be Scotland's King. He could not claim, like Wallace,

The Wallace Sword (*Reproduced from the Official Guide to the Wallace Monument by courtesy of the Stirling Town Council*)

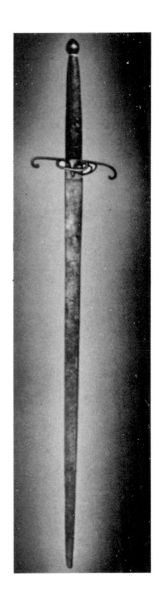

that he owed Edward no allegiance, for he had served that monarch and his name appeared on the Ragman Rolls. He was, additionally, in obscure conspiracy with William Lamberton, Bishop of St Andrews, an unscrupulous patriot operating in a labyrinth of duplicity. A sudden deed of violence forced Bruce to see his way clear. On 10 February 1306 he met John Comyn to confer alone in the church of the Grey Friars at Dumfries. A quarrel ensued and Bruce killed "the Red Comyn" with "sacrilegious blow".* He was now faced with two alternatives – he must fly the country or seize power. He chose the latter, roused a number of followers and, on 27 March 1306, was crowned with a plain band of gold before a small gathering at Scone.

* The deed is commemorated by a plaque on the wall of a supermarket in Castle Street, Dumfries.

Robert The Bruce – Bronze Statue by C. D'O Pilkington
Jackson at Bannockburn

(*National Trust for Scotland*)

ROBERT I (THE BRUCE), 1306–1329

(Son of Robert Bruce, Earl of Carrick and Annandale and Marjorie, Countess of Carrick. Grandson of Robert Bruce, "The Claimant" – see pages 81, 83, 90 – great-great-great-great-grandson of DAVID I)

Born 1274, was 31 when he ascended the throne, and 54 when he died.

Married Isabella of Mar – had one daughter: Marjorie, who married Walter, the High Steward.

Married Elizabeth de Burgh – had four children including: DAVID II

Thumbnail Sketch Personal ambition ruled his early career, but, proving himself great in war and policy, he became the Patriot King.

THE REIGN

The new monarch faced an unpromising situation. Excommunicated for a crime committed on holy ground, unacceptable to many of his compatriots as "that fell homicide The Bruce", he was no more than the precariously placed King of an enemy-occupied country. In June 1306 the Earl of Pembroke, Edward's commander in Scotland, defeated him at Methven, near Perth, and he fled to the forests, hills and islands – traditionally hunted by hounds and encouraged by spiders. Within eight months the women of his family were imprisoned, three of his brothers had been executed, and the Countess of Buchan, who had crowned him at Scone, was incarcerated in a cage. Early in 1307 he made a come-back in the West. He was victorious in Glen Trool, ten miles north of Newton Stewart, in March, and in May he avenged Methven by defeating Pembroke on the great rocky hump of Loudon Hill, east of Kilmarnock. It now seemed that he would have to face the full might of England but, providentially for him, Edward I died in camp at Burgh-by-Sands, just south of the Solway, on 7 July.

The "Hammer of the Scots" had left macabre death-bed

instructions that his bones should be carried over the border at the head of the army. His son, however, the foolish Edward II, gave up the campaign and turned south to enjoy frivolous pursuits in the company of attractive young men. Bruce was thus free to conquer his kingdom, which meant the suppression of the Balliol-Comyn Fifth Column, and the capture and destruction of the castles from which the English had ruled the country. The work went forward systematically and successfully with the assistance of the King's brother Edward Bruce, his nephew Thomas Randolph and Sir James Douglas (the famous "Black Douglas" whose dreaded name was used by English mothers to quell their rebellious children). By 1311 it was possible to raid England and, by 1313, Stirling Castle alone remained in enemy hands. There Edward Bruce agreed with Sir Philip Mowbray, its commander, that the place should be surrendered if not relieved by an English force before midsummer 1314.

This seemingly absurd arrangement brought Edward II north with 20,000 men. Bruce, with something like 7,000, awaited Edward near Bannockburn, on terrain of his own choosing. The engagement of 24 June 1314 ended in decisive victory for the smaller force, and with the defeated Edward riding ingloriously for Dunbar. It had been a triumph of leadership, discipline, battle experience and use of ground, which dispirited the English and determined Scottish waverers to throw in their lot with Scotland's King.

But it was still necessary that the King *de facto* be recognized by England and the Pope as the King *de jure* of an independent country. To achieve this Bruce began, in his turn, to "hammer" the English with frequent raids, including a diversionary expedition to Ireland, where Edward Bruce became monarch in 1317, only to be killed a year later. Edward had been named as heir to

the Scottish throne so now a succession problem arose. It was decided that, should the King die without surviving children, the crown would pass to Robert, son of Bruce's daughter Marjorie. She had married Walter, the

Boss of the Bannatyne or Bute Mazer

(By courtesy of the Marquess of Bute, on loan to the National Museum of Antiquities of Scotland)

High Steward of Scotland, from whom the name Stewart came. But in 1324 the child who would be David II was born, and a new deal was necessary. A parliament met at Cambuskenneth in 1326 (this was the first occasion on which the burghs had been invited to send representatives) and swore allegiance to Bruce's son as heir. Robert Stewart was now relegated to second place and would take over if David died childless. Not surprisingly there was little love lost between these two.

The mettle of the country had already been shown by the Declaration of Arbroath of 1320. This noble confession of faith in Scotland's nationhood and love of liberty,* addressed to Pope John XXII, must have impressed as its resounding Latin rolled round the great hall of the *Palais des Papes* at Avignon. But it was not until 1328 that the ban of excommunication on Bruce was lifted. In the same year England's disreputable Queen Isabella, and her lover Mortimer, having deposed – and, indeed, disposed of – Edward II, acknowledged Bruce's claims and agreed that his son David should marry Joanna, sister of Edward III. Next year Bruce died at Cardross, possibly of leprosy. He lies, like St Margaret, in the Parish Church at Dunfermline (see page 73).

* "It is not for glory, riches or honour that we fight; it is for liberty alone, the liberty which no good man loses but with his life."

David II and Edward III, from an illuminated fourteenth-
century manuscript

(*By courtesy of the Trustees of the British Museum*)

DAVID II, 1329–1371

(Son of ROBERT I – THE BRUCE – and Elizabeth de Burgh)

Born 1324, was 5 when he ascended the throne, and 46 when he died.

Married Joanna, daughter of Edward II of England. No issue.
Married Margaret Logie. No issue.

Thumbnail Sketch Pleasure loving, perhaps, but courageous and charming. When finally given a chance, in his thirties, he succeeded in dominating his kingdom.

THE REIGN

The Bruce had won independence and sovereignty for Scotland, symbolized when David II received "*anointing* and coronation" (authorized by Papal Bull) in November 1331 at Scone. But the essential element of leadership was lacking. The King was a child. "The dreadful blacke Douglas" had fallen in battle against the Moors in Spain – he had Bruce's heart * with him and hurled it at his enemies on a stricken field, whence it is said to have been recovered and buried at Melrose – and Thomas Randolph, Earl of Moray, appointed Guardian, died in 1332. At this moment Edward Balliol, John's son, landed at Kinghorn, on the northern shore of the Firth of Forth, supported by a number of nobles disinherited by Bruce for collaboration with the English. He defeated and killed the new Guardian (the Earl of Mar) at Dupplin, south-west of Perth. He had himself crowned at Scone, but was caught by a Scottish raid at Annan and galloped for the Border bareback and minus one boot. In 1333 he was back again with Edward III, besieging Berwick. In July a Scottish army marched to that town's relief but, at Halidon Hill, the long-bow proved irresistible once again, and the English were victorious.

Scotland's young King and Queen were now sent to safety in France, where they enjoyed the amenities of the Château Gaillard until 1341. Balliol was happy to perform as a feudal puppet,

* Hence the heart in the Douglas coat of arms.

manipulated by Edward III, and made over to his master a considerable area of the Southern Uplands. But there was a resistance movement, led by Sir Andrew Moray of Bothwell ("Black Agnes", the Countess of March, who defended Dunbar Castle, is its picturesque heroine), and Scotland was eventually saved from Balliol by Edward III's preoccupation with the Hundred Years War, waged sporadically by England and France from 1337 to 1453.

David and Joanna returned from France in 1341. The King, aged 17, was totally inexperienced in the art of governing, but was imbued with the militarily unrealistic doctrines of chivalry – doctrines which were to lose France the battles of Crécy, Poitiers and Agincourt. Confident in his unsound conception of soldiering, and true to his alliance with the French, he invaded England on their behalf in 1346. Some ten miles south-west of Durham he suffered a severe defeat at Neville's Cross, hardly redeeming his faulty tactics by courage and the two wounds he received before being taken prisoner.

For the next eleven years David underwent agreeable captivity in London and Hampshire. In Scotland Robert the Steward (son of Bruce's daughter Marjorie – see page 94) shouldered the thankless burden of regency, an English occupation was endured, the Black Death visited the land, and an attempt by the French to stimulate military activity against the common enemy caused Edward III to harry the country as far as Edinburgh in a

DUNFERMLINE

devastating foray picturesquely called "The Burnt Candlemas".

The miseries of this operation, in which his own troops had suffered greatly and which had earned him nothing but hatred and loss of prestige, probably influenced Edward's decision to release David in 1357 (Treaty of Berwick). The ransom was fixed at 100,000 marks, to be cleared by 1367, at the rate of 10,000 marks annually – and a truce between England and Scotland was declared. These demands

Glazed Earthenware Jug said to have been found in
Crail (1300–1400)
(National Museum of Antiquities of Scotland)

provided a motive for putting Scotland's financial house in order,
and remarkable results were achieved – though the contributions
paid to Edward were always irregular and never completed. The
money-making merchant class increased in importance, and it
was now that Scotland's parliament really took the form of "Three
Estates" – clergy, nobles and burgesses. The succession, too, presented problems, for the twice-married David achieved no legitimate issue. He disliked Robert the Steward, whose conduct at
Neville's Cross had been, at best, equivocal; and he had negotiated
with Edward III suggesting that the latter, or one of his sons,
might inherit the Scottish throne. This throw-back to the Treaty
of Birgham (see page 81), and forecast of 1603, when the crowns
of England and Scotland were united, does not seem entirely
despicable, but it did not command contemporary enthusiasm.
And there were discontented nobles to suppress, notably in 1363.
But when he died in Edinburgh Castle in 1371, David was, in
fact, dominating his kingdom.

Robert II – Great Seal

(*Mansell Collection*)

ROBERT II (STEWART), 1371–1390

(Son of Walter, High Steward of Scotland, and Marjorie daughter of ROBERT I – THE BRUCE – nephew of DAVID II)

Born 1316, was 54 when he ascended the throne, and 74 when he died.

Married Elizabeth Mure – had nine children including:
>John, Earl of Carrick – ROBERT III
>Robert, Duke of Albany
>Alexander, Earl of Buchan and Ross – "The Wolf of Badenoch".

Married Euphemia of Ross – had four children including:
>Walter, Earl of Athol

Thumbnail Sketch   An elderly noble who, despite previous experience, was unable to exert himself and rule, when the Kingship came his way.

THE REIGN

Robert II, the first Stewart King, was some eight years older than his uncle and predecessor. Of the fifteen monarchs hitherto recorded, ten had died, and one – John Balliol – had been deposed, before they were 55, the age at which Robert was crowned. His immediate concern was to assure the succession, and he rapidly achieved the acceptance, by his parliament, of John – eldest son of his union with Elizabeth Mure – as heir.

There followed, in 1372, the inevitable treaty with France, which meant a renewal of war with England. Crude hostilities of raid and counter-raid swung to and fro across the border in desultory, unplanned and fatiguing fashion during most of the reign. A climax of activity was reached in the mid-1380s when John of Gaunt, Duke of Lancaster, fourth son of Edward III, penetrated as far as Edinburgh, shortly after which a French expeditionary force landed in the Firth of Forth. This was commanded by John of Vienne, one of the military heroes of the Hundred Years War, who, though he was totally unacquainted with the sea, had built up a fleet and been rewarded with the rank of

Admiral of France. He and his men did not find operations in Scotland in any way agreeable – they were exceedingly unenthusiastic about such accommodation as was offered, and totally mystified by the Scots' technique of waging war. Withdrawal, after a short stay, came as a relief and made it easier for Richard II of England to undergo his first experience of campaigning by ingloriously ravaging certain Border Abbeys and Edinburgh.

In 1388 the great family of Douglas plunged cheerfully into that conflict with the Percys of Northumberland which is the subject of the ancient ballads of *Chevy Chase* and the *Battle of Otterbourne*. The Scots "invaded Northumberland; and, having wasted part of the county of Durham, advanced to the gates of Newcastle; where, in a skirmish, they took a 'penon' or colours belonging to Henry Lord Percy, surnamed Hotspur, son to the Earl of Northumberland." (*Percy's Reliques*) Hotspur pursued and surprised the enemy in their camp. "But James, Earl of Douglas, rallying his men, there ensued one of the best-fought actions that happened in that age; both armies showing the utmost bravery." (*Ibid.*)

"Thys fraye began at Otterbourne
By-twene the nyghte and the day:
Ther the Dowglas lost hys lyfe,
And the Percy was lede awaye."

(*Ibid.*)

DUNDONALD CASTLE

Despite this excursion into apparent romance the history of the later fourteenth century offers gloomy reading enough – plague and pestilence, public and private warfare, the Peasants' Revolt in England and a recrudescence of disturbances of the *Jacquerie* type in France. In Scotland suffering was, perhaps, particularly acute. South of the Highland Line overmighty subjects fought one another, when not engaged against the English. The High-

Loch an Eilean Castle (Rothiemurchus Forest) – once held
by the "Wolf of Badenoch"

(Scottish Tourist Board)

landers themselves – as they developed their clan system – special-
ized in family feuds, and when Robert II handed them over to his
son Alexander, Earl of Buchan and Ross, the latter earned the
terrifying nickname of "the Wolf of Badenoch", and burned Elgin's
splendid cathedral in 1390 to avenge the excommunication he
had brought upon himself by his matrimonial misdemeanours. Life
really was "nasty, brutish and short", except in the case of the
King who, when he died at his favourite castle of Dundonald,
west of Kilmarnock, in the spring of 1390, had achieved an age
greater than that of any Scottish ruler who had gone before him.
We owe him at least one debt. It was due to Royal patronage that
his exchequer auditor, John Barbour – Archdeacon of Aberdeen
and probably with experience of the universities of Oxford and
Paris behind him – was able to write his epic poem *The Bruce*
with its message, "loud as trumpets with a silver sound", that
"freedome is a noble thing".

Robert III – Great Seal

(Mansell Collection)

ROBERT III, 1390–1406

(Son of ROBERT II and Elizabeth Mure)

Born about 1337, was about 53 when he ascended the throne and about 69 when he died.

Married Annabella Drummond – had seven children including:
>   David, Duke of Rothesay
>   JAMES I

Thumbnail Sketch   A mild old gentleman of kindly virtues whose sombre self-assessment reads: "The worst of kings and most wretched of men."

THE REIGN

The successor of Robert II had been christened John – a name evocative of failure – for there was little inspiration in the histories of Scotland's John Balliol, England's John Lackland and John the Good of France who was captured at Poitiers. So the new monarch was crowned at Scone on 14 August 1390 under the more stimulating appellation of Robert III. A gentle and melancholy temperament, combined with the physical disability induced by a riding accident, made him unfit to rule, so his brother Robert, Earl of Fife, continued to exercise the function of Guardian of the Kingdom to which he had been elected in 1388.

The state of Scotland remained chaotic, with great families like the Douglases and the Macdonalds – the latter now virtually independent as Lords of the Isles – showing scant respect for the crown and total disregard for the law. The chronicles are full of "homicides, robberies, fire-raisings and other misdeeds". A climax was reached in 1396 with the famous Battle of the Clans on the North Inch at Perth – lovely scene of today's innocent diversions of cricket and football. Here, as readers of Scott's *The Fair Maid of Perth* will remember, two teams of thirty Highlanders each, probably representing the Chattans and the Kays, were invited to settle their differences in the presence of the King and an appreciative audience by hacking away at each other until some forty-nine fatal casualties had been achieved – without making any significant contribution to the good order of the realm.

Shortly after this picturesque, if bloody, event Scotland's first two Dukedoms were instituted by Robert III. His brother the Earl of Fife was created Duke of Albany and his son David – the heir apparent – became Duke of Rothesay (a title held by the Prince of Wales to this day). Albany then faded temporarily into the background while Rothesay was given the appointment of King's Lieutenant and charged with ruling the country for three years. His intelligence and ability were more than offset by a profligacy which earned him powerful enemies. He had, of course, acquired one already in his uncle of Albany, who was naturally chagrined at being superseded. He added another in the Earl of March, by breaking a betrothal contract with his daughter, which caused that outraged nobleman to leave for England and find favour at the court of Henry IV. Finally, having married Marjorie, sister of the fourth Earl of Douglas, he incensed the latter by the irresponsible infidelity to which he swiftly subjected his bride. In 1400 Henry IV invaded Scotland, without great effect, and the inadequate Rothesay was arrested and imprisoned at Falkland early in 1402. He died in March. Hector Boece and Sir Walter Scott fostered the tradition that he was starved to death at the instance of Albany – the truth remains obscure.

The North Inch, Perth (Battle of The Clans, 1396)

(A. C. Cowper and Co., Perth)

Meanwhile the English war continued with another Douglas-Percy combat. This time the action took place at Homildon Hill, near Wooler in Northumberland, where Hotspur had his revenge for Otterbourne. Douglas, who was taken prisoner, made common cause with his captors when the latter fell out with Henry IV about his ransom. He went off with them to support the rebellion which "the great magician, damned Glendower" was leading in Wales and thus shared in their defeat on "a bloody field near

Shrewsbury" in 1403. He was captured again and did not return to Scotland until 1409.

Three years prior to this the final tragedy of Robert III's reign had occurred. The monarch, fearing for the safety of his eleven-year-old heir (later James I), had decided to send him to France. The boy embarked secretly from the Bass Rock in a ship of Danzig – but was picked up by English buccaneers off Flamborough Head on 22 March 1406 and transported to the English court, where he was to remain for 18 years. The news of his capture contributed to the death of his father, which took place at Dundonald on 4 April 1406.

TOWARDS CENTRAL GOVERNMENT
1406–1542

James I	1406–1437
James II	1437–1460
James III	1460–1488
James IV	1488–1513
James V	1513–1542

In England		*In France*	
Henry IV	1399–1413	Charles VI	1380–1422
Henry V	1413–1422	Charles VII	1422–1461
Henry VI	1422–1461	Louis XI	1461–1483
Edward IV	1461–1470	Charles VIII	1483–1498
Henry VI (restored)	1470–1471	Louis XII	1498–1515
Edward IV	1471–1483	Francis I	1515–1547
Edward V	1483		
Richard III	1483–1485		
Henry VII	1485–1509		
Henry VIII	1509–1547		

Renaissance Façade at Falkland Palace, added by James V

(National Trust for Scotland)

TOWARDS CENTRAL GOVERNMENT
1406-1542

Anyone who has hitherto entertained the erroneous idea that Scotland is poor in architecture must, by now, be reconsidering his or her views. The fifteenth and sixteenth centuries produced a great number of Tower Houses – a name generally descriptive of the smaller fortified dwellings – and a mass of castles. Shakespeare will no doubt inspire you to take a look at the Keep of Cawdor (but you will recollect that it was built in the mid-fifteenth century, some 400 years after the death of Macbeth). Similarly Scott may tempt you to Craignethan, 4 miles down the Clyde from Lanark, whose ruins have "something of the character" of Tillietudlem in *Old Mortality*. And then, of course, there is extremely important Renaissance work at Stirling and at the palaces of Linlithgow and Falkland.

Ecclesiastical buildings which have been mentioned before – like Melrose – develop further with lovely fifteenth-century ornament, and a great vogue now arises for the foundation of collegiate churches by men of substance, anxious for the felicity of their immortal souls. Prominent among these are Seton, Rosslyn (described by Mr H. V. Morton as "the most ornate piece of Gothic in the British Isles") and the Parish Kirk at Crichton (all within 15 miles of Edinburgh).

Amateurs of bridges should be on the alert at Aberdeen, Guard Bridge (near St Andrews), Dumfries and Ayr, and those who share Goethe's eminently tenable view that Robert Burns was "the first of lyric poets" will gladly move three miles south of the last named town to see Alloway's enchanting Auld Brig o' Doon.

James I – Artist unknown

(*Scottish National Portrait Gallery*)

JAMES I, 1406–1437

(Son of ROBERT III and Annabella Drummond)

Born 1394, was 11 when he succeeded and 42 when he was murdered.

Married Joan Beaufort – had eight children including:

JAMES II

Margaret – married the Dauphin, later ⎤
    Louis XI of France, but died before his
    accession   ⎟ These marriages indi-
Isabella – married Duke Francis II of ⎬ cate the growing im-
    Brittany   ⎟ portance of Scotland
Eleanora – married Duke Sigismund of ⎟ in Europe.
    Austria
Mary – married the Count of Grandpré ⎦

Thumbnail Sketch A scholar, poet, athlete and statesman whose precipitancy, ruthlessness and love of grandeur led him to a violent death.

THE REIGN

Scotland's new King was a boy and a prisoner. The country remained in the hands of Albany, who appeased overmighty subjects by letting them make holiday on increasingly vast properties surrounded by ever-growing bands of retainers. Nevertheless when, in 1411, Donald, Lord of the Isles, stormed east to seize the Earldom of Ross (in the area of the Dornoch and Moray Firths) he was halted at Harlaw, north-west of Aberdeen, by Albany's nephew the Earl of Mar, son of the "Wolf of Badenoch". In 1412 a more agreeable note was struck in the foundation of St Andrew's university and in 1420 Albany died, full of years if not of honour. He was succeeded by his son Murdoch, who shared the family's lack of enthusiasm for the return of James I, which nevertheless occurred in 1424. Henry V had died and the English thought that James's release might stop the assistance which the Scots were giving to the French. A formidable bill for his eighteen years' schooling and maintenance was presented – but never wholly paid.

James, a highly educated and extremely tough young man, had had some experience of affairs in peace and war. He knew about English government and had seen service in France where Henry V produced him at his side to suggest that the Scottish contingent with the French was fighting against its lawful monarch. He had also made a love-match with Joan Beaufort, daughter of the Earl of Somerset and granddaughter of John of Gaunt – heroine of James's poem *The Kingis Quair* (King's Book). Bride and bridegroom crossed the border early in April 1424 and were crowned at Scone on 21 May.

Captivity is conducive to meditation and James's plan for Scotland was to "make the key keep the castle and the bracken bush the cow" – that is to enforce order on all classes. He regarded his long captivity as the fault of the House of Albany, and twelve months had barely passed when the Duke, two of his sons and his father-in-law the Earl of Lennox were executed for high treason upon the Heading Hill at Stirling (1425). In 1427 wholesale arrests and three executions disciplined the Highland chiefs during a parliament at Inverness. In 1429 a quarrel with Alexander Macdonald, new Lord of the Isles, culminated in the latter's surrender during Mass at Holyrood, dressed as a penitent and carrying his sword by the point. 1430 saw the imprisonment of the fifth Earl of Douglas, and 1435 the dispossession of the Earl of March becuase of his father's defection in 1400 (see page 106).

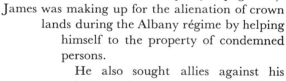

James was making up for the alienation of crown lands during the Albany régime by helping himself to the property of condemned persons.

He also sought allies against his nobility in the commons of Scotland. He probably favoured an English type of parliament and certainly tried to push his country's estates towards that model. But the lesser feudatories showed no desire to attend and even when James absolved them from their obligations and demanded instead the appearance of two commissioners per shire, and also

ST SALVATOR'S COLLEGE,
ST ANDREWS

Gold Signet Matrix of Queen Joan (Beaufort)

(National Museum of Antiquities of Scotland)

representatives from the royal burghs, these humble folk, if they came at all, sat mum in the presence of their betters, longing only for the day when they might return home.

Nevertheless the reign's flood of legislation would largely have done credit to an eighteenth-century enlightened despot. It touched on commerce, currency, beggars, archery, salmon, agriculture and the depredations of crows, wolves and poachers. Furthermore an attempt was made to combat the law's delays by the creation of a committee which was to develop into Scotland's supreme court, the Court of Session, while church discipline was encouraged by the foundation of a Charterhouse (monastery of the strict Carthusian order) at Perth.

But there were those who found the monarch's yoke uneasy, which gave an opportunity to Walter, Earl of Athol (see page 101) who (as son of Robert II by Euphemia Ross) saw himself as legitimate King of Scotland, whereas James was descended from Elizabeth Mure whose tardy marriage with Robert was not held by all to have expunged the previous bastardy of her children. Athol, his grandson Sir Robert Stewart and the disgruntled Sir Robert Graham encompassed the assassination of James I at Perth on 21 February 1437.

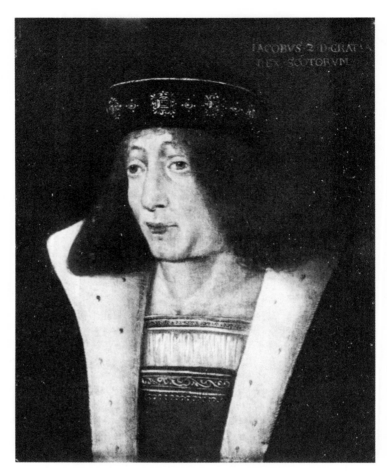

James II – Artist Unknown

(*Scottish National Portrait Gallery*)

JAMES II, 1437–1460

(Son of JAMES I and Joan Beaufort)

Born 1430, was 6 when he ascended the throne and 29 when he was killed.

Married Mary of Guelders – had eight children including:
> JAMES III
> Alexander, Earl of March, Duke of Albany
> John, Earl of Mar
> Mary – married Sir Thomas Boyd,
>> married James, Lord Hamilton (Henry Stewart, Lord Darnley, who married Mary Queen of Scots, was great-great-grandson of this marriage)

Thumbnail Sketch James "of the Fiery Face" (so called from a birthmark) had gifts of charm and leadership. Though less of an intellectual than his father he had the same ruthlessness and followed the same path.

THE REIGN

March 1437 saw the coronation of the six-year-old King at Holyrood. In the same month a ghastly parody of that ceremony took place in Edinburgh's Grassmarket when, it is said, Athol's brow was encircled with red-hot iron before he was beheaded. Nor were the other assassins of James I allowed an easy death.

Archibald, 5th Earl of Douglas, was appointed Regent. Despite the riches and grandeur of the great (and indeed international) Black Douglas family, with their broad acres in Scotland and lordships in France, the Earl proved a man of straw. When he died in 1439 Sir William Crichton (Keeper of Edinburgh Castle) and Sir Alexander Livingston (his Stirling counterpart) fought for the custody of James II, in the course of which struggle Livingston imprisoned the Queen Mother and her new husband.* But, realizing that the Douglas power blocked their ambitions, the two knights allied and invited the new sixteen-year-old Earl of Douglas

---

* Sir James Stewart of Lorne. They had three sons. The Queen Mother died at Dunbar in 1445.

to dine in Edinburgh Castle with his brother and a companion. Sir Walter Scott writes that, at the end of the repast, "the head of a black bull was put on the table . . . the sign of death" and the three young men were killed, despite the King's protests. Chaos ensued. The 7th Earl of Douglas, who may have welcomed this murder of his great-nephew, died in 1443. Livingston, a believer in "the big battalions", threw in his lot with the 8th Earl – as powerful as any of his predecessors by reason of heredity and marriage – while Crichton allied himself with the saintly Bishop Kennedy of St Andrews. There followed six years of raid, counter-raid, siege, sack and excommunication – with a renewal of war on the border for good measure.

In 1449 James II married the cultivated and religious Mary of Guelders, a relative of the ducal house of Burgundy, and this seems to have changed the boy into a man. He immediately removed the Livingston menace by imprisonment and execution, and probably appreciated that the precipitation of a Douglas crisis was only a matter of time. In 1450 he invaded Douglas territory while the Earl was in Rome, but made an apparent reconciliation with this formidable subject on his return. He had reason to be suspicious, however, of Douglas's alliance with his three brothers and the Earl of Crawford, and invited him to Stirling in 1452, under safe-conduct, to discuss the matter. But Douglas proved intransigent, James drew his dagger and stabbed

ST MARY'S COLLEGE,
ST ANDREWS

him – the murder was completed by enthusiastic courtiers. At once the hunt was up as the 9th and last Earl sprang to arms and pronounced the monarch an outlaw. Parliament, on the other hand, recorded its opinion that "the Earl was guilty of his own death by resisting the King's gentle persuasion", and James followed the Roman Senate's dictum: "Divide and rule". Thus it was that the Douglas combination, with little support, was defeated at Arkin-

Female Head in Sandstone from Linlithgow Palace

(National Museum of Antiquities of Scotland)

holm near Langholm (Dumfriesshire) in 1455. The great title lapsed, though we shall hear again of the "Red" Douglases, who were Earls of Angus and descended from a bastard of William, the 1st "Black" Earl (1327–1384). Two sparks of light enliven the gloom of this period – the foundation in 1450 of St Salvator's College at St Andrews by Bishop Kennedy and, in 1451, of the University of Glasgow by Bishop Turnbull.

The years 1455 to 1460 were spent in the consolidation of royal power – a process well understood by James both politically and militarily. In the latter sphere he was an enthusiastic gunner, as the design of Ravenscraig Castle (Kirkcaldy – 1460) is held to show. England's involvement in the Wars of the Roses (1455–1485) offered an opportunity for the recapture of the stronghold of Roxburgh, which had been in enemy hands for over a century. On 3 August 1460 the King was watching a "bombard" battering at the fortress walls when the weapon exploded and killed him. In the grounds of Floors Castle, near Kelso, a holly tree is alleged to indicate the site of this disaster.

James III – From the Trinity Altar Piece by Hugo van der Goes

(Reproduced by Gracious Permission of Her Majesty the Queen)

JAMES III, 1460–1488

(Son of JAMES II and Mary of Guelders)

Born 1451, was 9 when he ascended the throne and 36 when he was murdered.

Married Margaret of Denmark – had three sons:
JAMES IV
James, Marquis of Ormonde, Duke of Ross, Archbishop of St Andrews *
John, Earl of Mar

Thumbnail Sketch A King whose unconventional interests – crafts, arts, sciences and the occult – led him to seek intellectual friends (not necessarily aristocratic) and distracted him from the business of ruling.

THE REIGN

The times became increasingly complicated. "Early Renaissance" ideas were abroad – embraced by some, opposed by others and ignored by many. A literature was emerging. We have already noted John Barbour and James I; the fourteenth century produced historians in John Fordun and Andrew of Wyntoun. This reign saw the poet Robert Henryson and something of William Dunbar – two members of quite a "nest of singing birds". It was a period of craftsmen and artists with architecture beginning to minister rather more to comfort and slightly less to defence, and wealth shown by a fine crop of churches. There was a mysterious inflationary crisis, but it was whispered that the King was managing to amass bullion. *Malaise* grew and in 1488 James was murdered, yet it was not a clear issue of nobility against crown, nor was it the old problem of the overmighty subject. Rather it seems that some of the aristocracy had fumbled their way to the conclusion that the monarch, despite parliamentary exhortations, was not doing his job.

Initially government was exercised by the statesman-prelate James Kennedy of St Andrews, who, favouring the Lancastrians

* Archbishopric since 1472.

in the English "Roses" struggle, granted asylum to Henry VI and Margaret of Anjou in 1461, accepting Berwick from them in return. This led Edward IV to encourage his guest, the exiled 9th Earl of Douglas, to combine with John, 4th and last Lord of the Isles and 12th Earl of Ross, in an abortive project to seize power in Scotland and then divide the country with Ross ruling north of the Forth and Douglas restored to his estates in the South, both as Edward's vassals. However, by the time Kennedy died in 1465, he had achieved a diplomatic understanding with England and the situation seemed stable.

But his death precipitated a familiar minority crisis. The Boyd family (Lord Boyd, his son Sir Thomas and his brother Sir Alexander) seized the young King. Thomas wed James's sister Mary and Lord Boyd brought off a *coup* in arranging James's marriage with the lovely daughter of Christian I of Denmark – stipulating that if her dowry were not paid Orkney and Shetland should become Scottish, which occurred in 1472. Yet the Boyd power did not survive this match (1469). In the absence of Sir Thomas to fetch the bride, and of Lord Boyd in England, James was influenced against the family. Sir Thomas, warned by his wife, escaped discreetly to Denmark in the ship which had brought Princess Margaret to Leith, Lord Boyd left England for the continent and Sir Alexander was executed.

CRAIGMILLAR CASTLE

The King's character now began to show itself and, despite a truce with England (1474) and the subjection of the Lord of the Isles (1476), there was discontent. James imprisoned his two brothers, whom he may well have had reason to distrust, but the elder – the Duke of Albany – made a dramatic escape from Edinburgh Castle while the younger – the Earl of Mar – incarcerated at Craigmillar, died in circumstances regarded by some as suspicious. In 1482 Albany invaded Scotland, accompanied by Richard of Gloucester (later Richard III of England). The King marched to

The Lamont Harp (1464)

(National Museum of Antiquities of Scotland)

meet him, followed by certain recalcitrant nobles, led by the "Red Douglas", Archibald 5th Earl of Angus, who caught him up at Lauder and there hanged a number of his artist-craftsmen friends from the bridge. All then withdrew to Edinburgh where Albany became Lieutenant General of the Kingdom, but left hurriedly in 1483, when his relations with Edward IV became too anglophile for his compatriots to stomach. He made an unsuccessful foray to Lochmaben, between Dumfries and Lockerbie, in 1484 * and was killed in a French tournament next year. Meanwhile Gloucester had taken Berwick (1482) which remained forever English. Eventually, in 1488, the powerful Home family, incensed at their loss of the revenues of Coldingham Priory to the King, incited other disgruntled notables to join them in rebellion. Using the fifteen-year-old Prince James as their figurehead, they defeated James III at Sauchieburn, near Bannockburn, on 11 June. Later that day, as the King lay injured by a fall from his horse, he appears to have been murdered.

* The 9th Earl of Douglas accompanied him, was captured and died in confinement at Lindores Abbey in 1488.

James IV – Artist Unknown

(Scottish National Portrait Gallery)

JAMES IV, 1488–1513

(Son of JAMES III and Margaret of Denmark)

Born 1472, was 15 when he ascended the throne and 40 when he was killed.

Married Margaret Tudor – had six children including:
> JAMES V (JAMES VI of Scotland and I of England was great-grandson of JAMES IV and Margaret Tudor.)

Thumbnail Sketch   Chivalrous and enquiring, devout and pleasure-loving, this immensely lively monarch and great leader was a transitional character from the Middle Ages to the Renaissance.

THE REIGN

Children matured fast in days when the expectation of life was short and soon James could rule in fact as well as name.

"Ane belt of irone", worn next the skin to keep green the guilty memory of his father's death, in no way impeded the King's amours. "Lightly from fair to fair he flew", applauded by his people. Similarly his frequent pilgrimages, with the same penitential motive, kept him in the public eye and were not rendered disagreeable by any austerity of travel arrangements.

This mild medievalism was offset by certain qualities of the Renaissance Prince. James, speaking Latin, Gaelic and five European languages in addition to his native tongue, had an Athenian delight in any new thing, whether it was the eccentric alchemist John Damian of Tongland crashing from Stirling's battlements on home-made wings, or Scotland's first printing-press, set up by Walter Chapman and Andrew Millar in 1507. In 1496 an optimistic Education Act laid down, without complete success, compulsory schooling in Latin for upper-class boys, who were then to proceed to a degree in law. Nor, with this intellectual activity, was the body neglected for, in 1505, Edinburgh acquired a College of Surgeons. In the world of letters Robert Henryson and William Dunbar continued their activities, Henry the Minstrel ("Blind Harry") celebrated Wallace, Gavin Douglas translated the *Aeneid* while John Major (though not in the Renaissance swim) was modern enough, in his *History of Greater Britain,* to see the sense of Anglo-Scottish union. Edinburgh, following the trend of James II's reign, became the unchallenged capital when the King built the Palace of Holyroodhouse hard by David I's abbey. Increased comfort and beauty is also discernible at Linlithgow, Falkland and elsewhere. And these new amenities were no Royal monopoly, for the reign saw a marked development in trade and commerce, bringing a new wealth which, though still eclipsed by that of France and England, made possible a real advance in material civilization. Furthermore James, an immensely travelled man within his kingdom, led his subjects to a new respect for law and, utilizing his charm and knowledge of the Gaelic, even attempted to control the Highlands and Islands by means of armed progresses – which led, above all, to the final subjection of the Lord of the Isles. The gap thus created facilitated the rise of the Campbells, Mackenzies and Gordons and, despite the notable backing given by the clans at Flodden, the King's writ did not really run among "the Wild Scots" until the latter half of the eighteenth century. Nonetheless the country described by the Spanish ambassador, Pedro de Ayala, in 1496 had advanced greatly from that pictured by Aeneas Sylvius Piccolomini (subsequently Pope Pius II) in 1435.

The reign, until 1512, saw technical peace with England except for the years 1495–1497, when James supported the pretender Perkin Warbeck against Henry VII. But that cautious monarch, intent on consolidating the young Tudor dynasty, was eager to secure his Scottish flank – hence the momentous marriage in 1503 between James and Henry's daughter Margaret. This union, however, did not prevent an undeclared naval war which lasted from 1504 to 1512, and, by exasperating James against his English neighbour, played its part in his final disaster.

Model of Sailing Ship *Great Michael*. Built 1511, 240 feet long,
36 feet broad within walls, 10 feet thick in the wall, 112 guns

(The Royal Scottish Museum, Edinburgh. Crown Copyright reserved)

In 1511 the warrior Pope Julius II formed a combination of
power politicians, miscalled the Holy League, to oppose the
expansionist policies of Louis XII of France. The ebullient young
Henry VIII of England joined the League, eager for martial
glory. Louis naturally invoked the traditional Auld Alliance and
invited James to draw off English troops by a northern diversion.
Nothing loth, James marched south to meet the Earl of Surrey
and to die, with many of his compatriots, at "Dark Flodden"
on 9 September 1513. "The Flowers of the Forest are a' wede
away," wrote Miss Elliot more than two hundred years later and,
in 1910, a granite cross was raised on the battlefield "To the Brave
of Both Nations".

James V – Artist Unknown
(*Scottish National Portrait Gallery*)

JAMES V, 1513–1542

(Son of JAMES IV and Margaret Tudor)

Born 1512, was 1 when he ascended the throne and 30 when he died.

Married Madeleine, daughter of Francis I of France. No issue.
Married Mary of Lorraine – had three children including:
MARY, Queen of Scots

Thumbnail Sketch   Under-educated, but demonstrating his architectural taste at Stirling, Linlithgow, Edinburgh and Falkland, this sensual and avaricious despot was "the Ill-Beloved" to his nobility and "the Goodman of Ballengeich" to the commonalty.

THE REIGN

An infant now succeeded, reviving the familiar problems of regency. James IV, by will, had appointed Queen Margaret as *tutrix*, while she remained a widow. This sultry sister of Henry VIII was not universally popular. Many favoured, as Regent, John Stewart, Duke of Albany, nephew of James III and son of the trouble-maker of that reign. Fortunately for her opponents, Margaret shared the *penchant* for marriage of her brother Henry VIII and forfeited her position in 1514 by a match with the chief of the Red Douglases, Archibald, 6th Earl of Angus, whom she soon found extremely uncongenial. So, in 1515, Albany replaced her as Regent – a firm, sensible ruler, though totally French by education. For the next nine years his movements between Scotland and France (his absences always left Scotland a prey to violence) were dictated by the diplomacy of François Premier and Henry VIII – the Auld Alliance being important to the former only when relations with the latter were strained. On Albany's first return to France in 1517 he negotiated the Treaty of Rouen – renewing the Alliance and envisaging a French marriage for James V. This agreement was confirmed in 1521 after the unsuccessful "Field of Cloth of Gold" summit between Francis and Henry. Albany twice led an army to the border (1522–1523) but the shadow of Flodden lay dark upon Scotland and there was no desire to sacrifice further Flowers of the Forest on the altar of Franco-Scottish friendship.

Albany left Scotland for good in 1524 and the boy-King found himself, once again, in his mother's hands. Despite his "installation" at Edinburgh, power lay between Margaret, her husband and the Earl of Arran.* In 1526, however, she divorced the incompatible Angus and married Henry. Stewart of Methven, which enabled her former husband to achieve complete control of his stepson. The Red Douglases ruled Scotland until June 1528, when James V escaped from Falkland Palace and rallied a powerful anti-Angus party at Stirling. The Earl resisted in his castle at Tantallon, near North Berwick, and was eventually allowed to leave for England. Broad Douglas acres were forfeit to the crown.

James embarked upon mastering his kingdom with fierce pleasure. With a "graceless face" he hanged the border freebooter, Johnnie Armstrong – and some of his adherents – in 1530. In the western highlands he disciplined the Earl of Argyll and, in 1532, streamlined the Court of Session (see page 115) as the College of Justice, thus reducing the law's delays. Many nobles regarded these moves, and the fact that the power of the crown was backed by financial aid from the church, with marked lack of enthusiasm.

FALKLAND PALACE

* Son of Princess Mary and James, Lord Hamilton – see page 117.

The Crown of Scotland remodelled by order of James V

(Crown Copyright. Reproduced with the permission of the Controller of Her Majesty's Stationery Office)

Humble folk, however, relished the King's amorous excursions into low life under various disguises.

Henry VIII, whose battle with the Papacy had started in 1529 wished James to follow his example. James, anglophobe because of his stepfather's predilection for England, retained the old faith and persecuted Lutheran heretics. But he enjoyed Sir David Lindsay's *Satyre of the Three Estates* in which the church in Scotland, deplorably rich and not notably dedicated to feeding its hungry sheep, was mercilessly pilloried. What the King required was money for himself and benefices for his bastards – claims upon which the Pope looked graciously in return for loyal orthodoxy.

Naturally James turned to "Most Christian" France for his bride. He married Madeleine, daughter of Francis I, in 1537. She died that year and his second wife (1538) was Mary of Lorraine, daughter of Claude, Duke of Guise, a family in the ascendant at the French court.

Henry VIII, displeased to see James thus bound to France, invited him to confer in York in 1541. But the Scottish King, elated perhaps by a voyage round his country from Leith to

Dumbarton in 1540, when he asserted his authority sharply over Highland and Island chiefs, failed to present himself. Much nettled, Henry despatched an army northward in 1542. Unsupported by his nobles, James sent a force under his favourite, Oliver Sinclair, to meet this threat. It was lost in the disastrous muddle of Solway Moss on 24 November. James, mourning the death of two infant sons in 1541, and sickened by this reverse, travelled to his beloved Palace of Falkland and died of a broken heart.

REFORMATION AND REACTION
1542–1603

Mary Queen of Scots. Part 1.	1542–1560
Part 2.	1561–1567
James VI Part 1.	1567–1603

In England		*In France*	
Henry VIII	1509–1547	Francis I	1515–1547
Edward VI	1547–1553	Henry II	1547–1559
Mary	1553–1558	Francis II	1559–1560
Elizabeth I	1558–1603	Charles IX	1560–1574
		Henry III	1574–1589
		Henry IV	1589–1610

Earl Patrick Stewart's Palace, Kirkwall, Orkney

(*Scottish Field*)

REFORMATION AND REACTION

1542–1603

You could base a sight-seeing tour on the romantic story of Mary, Queen of Scots. Edinburgh may kindle the imagination and you will meet the Queen again at Linlithgow, Stirling and Dumbarton. Also associated with her are the Lothian castles of Borthwick, Crichton and Craigmillar; on A1 are Dunbar and Hailes, and in the Border country lies the stronghold of Hermitage (to which Mary rode from Jedburgh, and back, on a day in 1566 when Bothwell lay wounded there). The Priory of Inchmahome, on the Lake of Menteith, sheltered her as a child; she hunted from Falkland Palace; she was imprisoned at Loch Leven (Kinross) and her last night in Scotland was spent in the Abbey of Dundrennan before she crossed the Solway Firth to Workington. In visiting these you will be looking at much medieval architecture again but seeing, too, further examples of the early Renaissance style, notably at Holyroodhouse, Edinburgh Castle, Stirling and Crichton.

Superb work of the period 1597–1603 is to be found at Huntly Castle, some 33 miles north-west of Aberdeen, and also at Kirkwall, where a singularly unpleasant Earl of Orkney, Patrick Stewart, son of one of James V's bastards, built himself a lovely palace, the ruins of which still stand.

The period 1542–1603 was one during which Scotland evolved a truly indigenous style of architecture based on the Tower House – without parallel in Europe – and which would reach its apogee with Craigievar, south of Alford – on A980 – in 1626. Meanwhile the splendid castle at Crathes, by Banchory on the Dee, was completed in 1596 and there was important building at Kellie Castle, 6 miles south of St Andrews, between 1573 and 1605. New churches, to suit new religious needs, began to appear – as at Burntisland, 1592, and, if you want to see "the whole life – religious, commercial and domestic – of a Scottish Royal Burgh of four centuries ago",* go to Culross on the north bank of the Forth, west of Dunfermline, which received its charter from James VI.

* *Culross. A Short Guide to the Royal Burgh.* The National Trust for Scotland.

Mary Queen of Scots – Artist Unknown

(Scottish National Portrait Gallery)

MARY (Queen of Scots), 1542–1567

(Daughter of JAMES V and Mary of Lorraine. Great-grand-
daughter of Henry VII of England through Margaret Tudor –
see page 125)

Born 1542, was a week old when she succeeded, 24 when she
abdicated and 44 when she was executed.

Married Francis II of France. No issue.
Married Henry Stewart, Lord Darnley. Had one son:
          JAMES VI of Scotland and I of England
Married James Hepburn, Earl of Bothwell. No issue.

Thumbnail Sketch   An attractive and passionate young woman of
undoubted courage and ability. Though devout and well educated she gravely lacked judgment in matters of men and affairs.

PART 1. THE REGENCIES. 1542–1560

The dying James V was told of his daughter's birth. He is
alleged to have remembered Marjorie Bruce and to have said:
"It cam' wi' a lass and it will gang wi' a lass." This was an
unwittingly true prophecy, for the crown passed from the House
of Stuart (Mary Queen of Scots spelt the name in the French
fashion) to that of Hanover on the death of Queen Anne. The
phrase also serves as a prelude to tragedy.

A Regent was appointed in James, 2nd Earl of Arran – son of
the 1st Earl (see page 130) and so grandson of the Princess Mary
who married James, Lord Hamilton (see page 117). As great-
grandson of James II he now became, at the age of twenty-seven,
heir to the fortnight-old Queen.

Arran faced a complicated situation. Henry VIII had already
made two wars against France since his accession and would
declare a third in 1544. Furthermore that monarch's ecclesiastical
manoeuvres had made it harder for England to find allies in a
mainly Roman Catholic Europe. Thus he was anxious to sweep
Scotland into the English religious and political orbit. He therefore sent north Archibald Douglas, Earl of Angus, in exile since
the end of resistance at Tantallon in 1528, together with certain

prisoners from Solway Moss, indoctrinated to sell the idea of marriage between Henry's son Prince Edward and Scotland's baby Queen. Enough of the latter's subjects entertained protes-tant and anglophile sympathies – including, in a vacillating manner, Arran himself – to permit the temporary realization of this policy in the Treaty of Greenwich (1543). There the match was agreed, Mary was to leave for England at the age of ten – and her compatriots were permitted to read the bible in Scots.

However, French influences were also at work. Many favoured the policy of the Auld Alliance and the maintenance of the ancient faith. This element was led by Mary of Lorraine, the Queen Mother, and Cardinal David Beaton, Archbishop of St Andrews – a man whose grasp of public affairs rendered him impressive as a statesman, even if the conduct of his private life was unbecoming in a prelate. This Lorraine–Beaton combination outmatched Arran, whose Greenwich policy was, therefore, rejected before the year closed. Henry VIII raged, and despatched the Earl of Hertford to Scotland on the notorious campaigns of 1544 and 1545 – known to history as "The Rough Wooing". This meant the devastation of the Border Abbeys and flames over Leith and Edinburgh, together with scores more villages and towns. In March 1546 Beaton added his own quota of violence by burning the reformer George Wishart, who was avenged within twelve weeks when the Cardinal's murdered body was hung out over the wall of St Andrews castle. His murderers and their adherents, sustained by the presence and sermons of a forty-one-year-old preacher named John Knox, then held the castle until the appearance of a French fleet in 1547, to which they surrendered and by which they were transported to serve in the Loire galleys. In the same year Hertford, now Duke of Somerset and Protector of England, reappeared in Scotland and defeated Arran at Pinkie, east of Edinburgh. The little Queen was whisked away to the safety of Inchmahome Priory, in the lake of Menteith, and – in 1548 – via Dumbarton to twelve happy years at the court of France. A French force was sent to assist Mary of Lorraine and in 1550, on the conclusion of the Anglo-French wars, English garrisons were withdrawn from Scotland with a guarantee that they would never molest that country again. The turn towards France, already clearly marked by 1548, when Arran was created Duke of Châtelherault in Poitou, was completed in 1554 when the Regency passed to Mary of Lorraine, nominated to that post by her twelve-year-old daughter.

The rule of the able and industrious Mary of Lorraine (1554–1560) is of enormous importance, above all because it embraces the Scottish Reformation. The country had already had experience of the Lutheran heresy and, with the accession of Mary Tudor in England (1553) further Protestants fled to Scotland, where they found the Roman Catholic Church presenting an unimpressive image. At the parish level there were poor and ignorant priests, in the upper strata there was wealth and ease, and throughout the hierarchy the progeny of bastards was remarkable for a body vowed to celibacy. It is true that between 1549 and 1559 genuine, if belated, attempts at internal church reform were made by Archbishop John Hamilton of St Andrews – Arran's illegitimate half-brother – who defended with vigour a faith which had little influence upon his morals. But the quality of his subordinates remained low and his ill-judged burning of the octogenarian Walter Myln in 1558 aroused an impressive measure of lay hostility.

Meanwhile in 1557 a number of evangelical reformers known as the "Lords of the Congregation" had bound themselves under the First National Covenant to replace the Roman Catholic by a Protestant church in Scotland. John Knox, toughened by the galleys, but now distinguished by having been a chaplain to Edward VI, and with the offer of an English bishopric, above all inspired by the theocracy of Calvin's Geneva, returned in 1559 to deploy the full power of his violent oratory. Iconoclastic riots followed at St Andrews, Scone, Perth, Stirling, Linlithgow and Edinburgh, and the Queen Mother's determination to impose discipline precipitated a civil war in which Lord James Stewart, a natural son of James V, commanded the reformers. The Protestants' obvious inability to make headway against Mary of Lorraine's French regular troops led them to send that extremely subtle statesman William Maitland of Lethington to negotiate help from Elizabeth I, Queen of England since November 1558. It was with reluctance that this vital, calculating female countenanced rebels – but here she had an impelling motive in that Roman Catholics abroad and in her own country saw her as the bastard of Henry VIII and Anne Boleyn, with Mary Queen of Scots, unimpeachably descended from Henry VII through Margaret Tudor, as rightful heir to the English throne. So an English army assisted the Congregation until on 10 June 1560 the Regent died in Edinburgh Castle, shortly after which her supporters surrendered at Leith. The Treaty of Edinburgh (or Leith) then concluded hostilities with the agreement that English and French troops should return home, that Mary Queen of Scots should remove the lions of England from the escutcheon displayed by herself and her husband Francis II of France,* and that a council should govern Scotland until such time as she herself might return.

A Scottish Parliament now turned with urgency to the religious problem. John Knox and his colleagues were swift to put before it a Confession of Faith – strange to many of his compatriots but acceptable to the Estates. The latter proceeded precipitately to deny the authority of the Pope, to declare the Mass illegal and to accomplish a root and branch reformation which contrasts interestingly with the step by step progress of England from Henry VIII's breach with Rome to the middle way church settlement of Elizabeth I. By the end of 1560 Presbyterianism, by no means fully fledged as yet, was certainly on its way. Here was Calvinism with all its virtues, including its emphasis on intellectual endeavour, and its vices – the merciless doctrine of predestination and the intolerable assurance of the Elect – poised to extend its grip over the land.

The scene was set for more than ordinary drama when a devout Roman Catholic Queen set foot on Scottish shores.

* Mary Stuart had married the French Dauphin in Notre Dame on 24 April 1558.

MARY (Queen of Scots), 1542–1567

PART 2. THE REIGN – 1561–1567

During Part I of the Mary Stuart drama great issues affecting Scotland's future had been at stake. The Calvinistic gloom with which the period closes is enlivened by the bright light of John Knox's educational ideal – that of a red carpet rolled out before the clever boy from parish school to university. This noble seed did not bear immediate fruit (in the 1560s too many people were interested in diverting the wealth of the old church into private pockets) but as the seventeenth century wore on the dream began to be realized and the glories of the eighteenth-century Scottish educational system, rooted in Knox's conception, were made possible.

The curtain rises on Part II of this drama at Leith, on 19 August 1561, when the lovely eighteen-year-old widow of Francis II of France steps ashore from the galley which has brought her from Calais. The stage is soon dominated by the swift-moving romance, passion and violence which characterizes the Elizabethan and Jacobean theatre.

Mary had hoped to visit Elizabeth of England on her way, but the safe-conduct was refused and no meeting ever took place – thus Mary's claim to the southern throne and the matter of her recognition as Elizabeth's heir remained undiscussed between the Queens. But in her native Scotland she was well received. Taking as her advisers Lord James Stewart, her half-brother (see page 139), and Maitland of Lethington, she disavowed any intention of interfering with the 1560 Reformation – reserving, however, the right to hear Mass in private – a determination which exposed her to the intolerable tirades of John Knox. More agreeable was a northern foray with Lord James to reduce the rebellious Gordons at Corrichie, near Banchory, in 1562 – after which Mary created her half-brother Earl of Moray.

In 1565 there appeared from England Mary's Catholic cousin Henry Stewart, Lord Darnley – like herself a grandchild of Margaret Tudor – in his case by that Queen's second marriage with Archibald 6th Earl of Angus (see page 129). This handsome, attractive boy was, in fact, a vicious light-weight, but he aroused a passion in Mary which obscured her judgment and led to their wedding within the year. Elizabeth was displeased at this reinforcement of English Royal blood about the Scottish throne while Moray, and certain other nobles, disliking Darnley's Romanism, took up arms. In the so-called "Chase-about Raid" Mary bustled them over the Border.

Wedded life with Darnley, however, soon showed the unattractive qualities of Dead Sea fruit. Though he bore the title of King, Mary witheld power from him and his frustrated jealousy focused on her confidential secretary David Riccio. Others who hated this luckless Piedmontese were the absent Moray's Protestant supporters, who plotted with the Queen's papist consort. On the night of 9 March 1566 they dragged Riccio from the Queen's presence at Holyrood and "twelve daggers were in him att once". One of these was Darnley's.

Mary now skilfully detached Darnley from his fellow-conspirators, pardoned the exiled Moray and his companions (who, whatever their sympathies, had not committed the murder) and, on 19 June, having survived the obvious dangers of miscarriage, gave birth to Darnley's son – later James VI of Scotland and I of England. In November she was conferring secretly at Craigmillar, near Edinburgh, about the desirability of ending her disastrous marriage with a husband who, at the close of the year, lay sick in Glasgow with small-pox or syphilis. In January 1567 Darnley was moved to a house on Edinburgh's outskirts called Kirk o' Field. Early on the morning of 10 February this building was shattered by an explosion, and the convalescent and a servant were found strangled in the garden. There were many who believed that James Hepburn, Earl of Bothwell, the strong man from the Border country who had increasingly aroused the Queen's interest since his support after the Riccio

LOCH LEVEN CASTLE

The Cadboll Cup

(National Museum of Antiquities of Scotland)

affair, was guilty of this most mysterious murder.

Folly was now heaped upon folly. After Bothwell's technical, but unimpressive, exoneration from the crime, and his indecently precipitate divorce, Mary took him as her husband on 15 May. A month later there followed, at Carberry Hill near Pinkie, a confrontation between her new consort's supporters and a force of rebellious nobles under the Earl of Morton. Mary persuaded Bothwell to escape from this affair, submitting herself to a short but humiliating incarceration in Edinburgh and subsequently in the island castle of Loch Leven. Her abdication followed on 24 July 1567, the coronation of her infant son came five days later and, by August, Moray was Regent.

The drama was not yet over. On 2 May 1568 Mary slipped out of Loch Leven but, despite Hamilton support, was defeated at Langside (now enveloped by southern Glasgow). Disastrously she sought asylum in England rather than France. From the Kirkcudbrightshire abbey of Dundrennan she crossed the Solway to Workington in Cumberland on 16 May. Her foot was irrevocably set on the road which would end at Fotheringay nearly twenty years later.

James VI, by Arnold Bronkhorst

(*Scottish National Portrait Gallery*)

JAMES VI OF SCOTLAND
and I OF ENGLAND, 1567–1625

(Son of MARY Queen of Scots and Lord Darnley. Great-great-grandson of Henry VII of England, through the latter's daughter Margaret Tudor – see page 125)

Born 1566, was 1 when he ascended the throne of Scotland, 36 when he ascended the throne of England and 58 when he died.

Married Anne of Denmark – had seven children including:
> Henry – died in 1612
> CHARLES I
> Elizabeth – married Frederick, the Elector Palatine, whose twelfth child, Sophia, became Electress of Hanover, to whom "and the heirs of her body being Protestant" the crown was to pass by the Act of Settlement of 1701.

Thumbnail Sketch A highly trained intelligence, combined with determination to survive and dominate, made him something more formidable than "the wisest fool in Christendom".

THE REIGN: PART 1. 1567–1603

With the coronation of James VI at Stirling on 29 July 1567 there started the tenth of those minorities which had bedevilled the Scottish monarchy since 1153. The period 1567–1578 saw four Regents. The first – Mary's half-brother, the "good" Earl of Moray * – fell victim to an assassination meticulously planned and executed at Linlithgow (January 1570) by James Hamilton of Bothwellhaugh, expressing the jealousy of the great house of Hamilton which had supported the ex-Queen at Langside.

For there was now in Scotland a Queen's party, opposing the current régime and plotting a restoration. It held the fortresses of Dumbarton and Edinburgh, formidable *points d'appui* for Civil War. Under Moray's successor – the Earl of Lennox (Darnley's father) – Dumbarton fell, but this Regent was killed at Stirling

---

* Not to be confused with his son-in-law "the bonny Earl", killed at Donibristle in 1592 and immortalized in *Percy's Reliques* as "the Queen's luve".

in September 1571. The Earl of Mar then took over, only to die in November 1572, within a few days of the demise of John Knox.

Government was now exercised by that tough power politician the Earl of Morton, whose task was rendered easier by the fact that the Parisian Massacre of St Bartholomew (August 1572) reduced the element of glamour attendant upon the possible return of the Catholic Queen. In 1573, aided by English artillery, Morton captured Edinburgh Castle, and the Queen's party ceased to exist. The Earl ruled on grimly until 1578, when the unpopularity caused by his sharp taxation, and the rigorous discipline imposed upon his fellow-aristocrats, led to his resignation.

A melodramatic figure now enters the Scottish scene from France. Esmé Stewart, Seigneur d'Aubigny, nephew of the late Regent Lennox, may have been the agent of an international papist conspiracy envisaging the rescue of Mary, a return to the ancient faith and the revival of the Auld Alliance – he certainly enchanted James. The thirteen-year-old King, whose motherless childhood had been devoted to rigorous education directed by the testy sexagenarian scholar George Buchanan – devotee of the classics and the rod – now found a gallant upon whom he rejoiced to lavish affection. He made him Earl, then Duke, of

The King's Bedchamber
at Falkland Palace with
the Golden Bed of Brahan

(The bed, which is Dutch,
dates from the reign of
James VI)

(*Country Life*)

Lennox. He ennobled the favourite's swashbuckling friend,
Captain James Stewart, as Earl of Arran. This pair then achieved
the execution of Morton (1581), for his connection with the Kirk
o' Field affair. The sinister idyll was, however, interrupted in
1582 by the Raid of Ruthven, when the Earl of Gowrie and other
nobles seized the monarch at the Ruthven stronghold of Hunting-
tower, near Perth, and ruled until James escaped in 1583,
whereupon Gowrie suffered death, while his confederates were
safely in England. Lennox had returned to France, but Captain
James Stewart soldiered on until the Ruthven Raiders came back
in force in 1585, under the aegis of Queen Elizabeth, and received
the royal pardon. He then fled and met, at last, an inevitably
violent end.

A major preoccupation of James was the matter of his succession to the English throne. This ensured that there was no violent
reaction on his part to his mother's execution in 1587, nor any
question of his helping Elizabeth's enemies during the Armada
menace of 1588. It also coloured his religious views, for the
Church of England, of which the monarch was "Supreme
Governor", suited his ambition to be "Universal King". His
consequent predilection for episcopacy resulted in a contest with
the Kirk (represented by Andrew Melville, a Calvinist theocrat,
second only in influence to the deceased John Knox) from which

James emerged victorious. There were bishops again in Scotland by 1603.

James had also come to believe in the absolutism which characterized the political climate of most of contemporary Europe. He set himself with devious subtlety, tactful conciliation and dogged perseverance to dominate the Scottish nobility, whose instinct was still to "bang it out bravely". This meant the suppression of the rebellion of the Catholic Earls (Huntly, Errol and Angus) in 1595, and the death of yet another Earl of Gowrie in the possibly seditious and certainly peculiar "Gowrie Conspiracy" of 1600. By 1603 James VI was master of Scotland.

THE DUAL MONARCHY
1603–1707

James VI and I. Part 2.	1603–1625
Charles I	1625–1649
Charles II and Cromwell	1649–1660
Charles II (Restored)	1660–1685
James VII and II	1685–1689
{William and Mary	1689–1694
{William III	1694–1702
Anne	1702–(1714)

In France

Henry IV	1589–1610
Louis XIII	1610–1643
Louis XIV	1643–1715

Courtyard—The Palace of Holyroodhouse 1671–1678.
By Sir William Bruce
(*Reproduced by permission of the Department of the Environment. Crown Copyright*)

THE DUAL MONARCHY
1603–1707

The seventeenth century was one of great building activity in Scotland, but it is difficult to trace any link-by-link architectural development. The indigenous style on the basis of the Tower House continued (its apogee with Craigievar in 1626 has already been noted) and there are good examples of this at Coxton Tower (1644), about three miles east of Elgin, and Leslie Castle (1661) some four miles south-west of Insch "at the back o' Bennachie".

In the early years of the seventeenth century there was a vogue for decorating old-fashioned buildings with new-style Renaissance ornament, and important work was accomplished at Edinburgh Castle and Linlithgow between 1615 and 1621. But there is nothing truly transitional to lead on from this to, e.g. Sir William Bruce's courtyard at Holyroodhouse (1671–1678) and Kinross House (1686–1689). It is as if God had said: "Let Bruce be!" and all was classicism, of which these two buildings are outstanding examples. Sir William (appointed King's Surveyor in Scotland, 1671) was also responsible for the church at Lauder (1673), designed primarily for Presbyterian worship. With similar intent the first Duke of Queensberry had the church at Durisdeer (at the foot of Dalveen Pass, between A74 and A76, just north of Thornhill) constructed at the end of the century.

Though you are unlikely to emulate Old Mortality and "annually visit the graves of the unfortunate Covenanters" you may well find interest in the memorials which perpetuate their saga at Rullion Green, Drumclog, Bothwell Bridge, Sanquhar, Aird's Moss and Wigtown.

And if horticulture is your line, do not miss the fine example of a restored seventeenth-century garden at the House of Pitmedden, 14 miles north of Aberdeen, originally laid out by Sir Alexander Seton, a judge who lost his appointment in 1686, as the result of opposing the religious policy of James VII and II.

James VI and I – artist unknown

(*Scottish National Portrait Gallery*)

JAMES VI OF SCOTLAND
and I OF ENGLAND, 1567–1625

THE REIGN: PART 2 – 1603–1625

James was in bed in Holyroodhouse on the evening of 26 March 1603 when a weary horseman, his head aching from a fall, clattered into Edinburgh. Sir Robert Carey had ridden hard for three days to accomplish this long-pondered mission. He brought the news that, in the small hours of 24 March, Elizabeth of England had died at Richmond Palace. Shortly after Carey's departure Sir Robert Cecil, the late Queen's Secretary of State, who had long been in touch with James, ensured the new King's proclamation in London.

On 5 April James left for the South – his "golf cloubbis" * emphasizing the holiday atmosphere which prevailed. Wine ran in the streets, crowds thronged the route, owners of great houses dispensed lavish hospitality and their guest revelled in unaccustomed affluence. On 7 May he reached London and took up residence at Greenwich. When joined by the Queen – a fretful blonde for whom his enthusiasm had diminished during fourteen years of matrimony – he took her to Windsor to avoid the bubonic plague which was abroad in the capital. This outbreak cast something of a gloom over the coronation, which nevertheless took place on 25 July in Westminster Abbey.

James had promised his Scottish subjects that he would return to his native land every three years – but flesh pots, friends and business meant that this undertaking was soon forgotten. The northern kingdom was governed through its own Privy Council directed by the King. This procedure flattered his absolutist pride: "I write, and it is done", he said, and the disciplining process continued. It was difficult to make the King's Writ run in the Highlands, where a record of bloody vendetta tended to obscure the attractions of poetry and the pipes, but the King did his best. Proceedings against the formidable Clan MacGregor had started

---

* Golf was a popular pastime with the Stuart monarchs from James IV to James VII and II – except for Charles II, who played the game without enthusiasm.

on 3 April 1603. These fierce men, probably as much sinned against as sinning, had massacred a number of Colquhouns in Glenfruin (near Helensburgh). For this they were condemned *en bloc* to outlawry, their name was suppressed and their chief hanged. Except for some years of respite granted by Charles II, rewarding them for services to his father, they remained under this ban until 1775 – by which time they had added another page to romantic history in the exploits of Rob Roy (1671–1734). Other clans to suffer were the Macdonalds and the Macleans; the cruel and tyrannous Patrick Stewart, Earl of Orkney, was executed; certain chiefs of the Western Isles signed the Statutes of Iona to guarantee peace in their territories, and comparative calm settled on the border.

James, attracted by the Church of England before his southward move, now sought to impose upon his northern subjects the blessings of Anglicanism – unwelcome to them. In 1605 the King forced certain recalcitrant ministers to leave Scotland, and a visit to London by Andrew Melville in 1606 resulted in the latter's imprisonment in the Tower for exercising his critical wit in verses about James's religious practices. (He left Great Britain in 1611 to take the chair of theology at Calvinist Sedan.) With Melville incarcerated it was possible to abolish Presbyterianism in Scotland, but it meant little to the ordinary Scottish churchgoer, whose worship remained plain and unadorned, that eleven bishops and two archbishops now directed his ecclesiastical affairs. In 1610 three of these travelled to England for consecration (with the benefits of the Apostolic Succession) and in the same year a Court of High Commission, on the English model, was introduced. Indignation was, however, caused in 1617 when James appeared personally (his only visit to Scotland after 1603) and the Chapel Royal at Holyrood witnessed the vanity of a surpliced choir whose voices were accompanied by organ music. This was followed in 1618 by the Five Articles of Perth requiring kneeling at communion, observance of the major feasts of the church, confirmation, private communion for the sick and early baptism. The Articles were widely ignored!

James's efforts to anglicize the Kirk are symptomatic of his desire for a United Kingdom – a concept unpopular on both sides

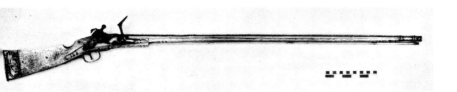

Sporting gun, of brass, made by James Low of Dundee in 1624
(National Museum of Antiquities of Scotland)

of the border and not to be achieved until 1707. Meanwhile Scots and English suffered the adoption of the appellation "Great Britain", the creation of the first Union Jack by the combination of the crosses of St Andrew and St George * and the right of those born after 1603 to citizenship of both countries – while the King presided over two independent and differing national administrations.

Scotland was the poorer of the two relations and, despite increased trade and manufacture, it was not easy to support 600,000 inhabitants. Scots went to Ulster, in 1621 an attempt was made to interest them in Nova Scotia (the lately invented title of Baronet was offered at £166 13s. 4d. to help finance that colonization†) and there were the attractions of continental soldiering – greatly increased by the Thirty Years War (1618–1648). However, by now Scotland had four universities (St Andrews 1411, Glasgow 1451, Aberdeen 1494, Edinburgh 1582) to England's two, the Knoxian educational ideal was on its way to fulfilment and John Napier of Merchiston published his invention of logarithms in 1614. But the most intellectual of Scottish Kings died in 1625 – weary and a failure in a foreign land.

* The cross of St Patrick was added in 1801 when the Parliaments of Great Britain and Ireland were united.

† N.B. The Nova Scotia Commemoration Room, Menstrie Castle, Clackmannanshire.

Charles I, Studio of Van Dyck

(Scottish National Portrait Gallery)

CHARLES I, 1625–1649

(Son of JAMES VI and I and Anne of Denmark)

Born 1600, was 24 when he ascended the throne, and 48 when he was executed.

Married Henrietta Maria of France – had eight children including:

>CHARLES II
>JAMES VII and II
>Mary – married William II of Orange
>Elizabeth
>Henry, Duke of Gloucester
>Henrietta – married Philip of Orleans

Thumbnail Sketch A formal, virtuous, cultivated absolutist inspired by High Anglican principles. He believed firmly that "a subject and a sovereign are clear different things".

THE REIGN

Charles I, though born in Dunfermline, "knew not the stomach" of the Scots. He applied to them his father's governmental technique, but aroused immediate hostility among the nobles by his determination to restore to the Church property which had passed into lay ownership with the Reformation. However in 1633 – by which time he had settled into eleven years of non-parliamentary government in England (1629–1640) – he was well received in Edinburgh, though the dignified ceremonial of his coronation in the church of St Giles was widely regarded as dangerously Popish. Four years later (23 July 1637) the same building was the scene of the famous "Jenny Geddes" riot, when a High Anglican prayer-book for Scotland – often miscalled "Laud's Liturgy", but largely compiled by Scottish bishops – was introduced.

This precipitated the National Covenant of 1638 whose signatories professed loyalty to Charles but refused to accept "novations" unauthorized by a free parliament and general assembly of the Kirk. The assembly, presided over at Glasgow later in the year by the formidable Alexander Henderson, disregarded its dissolution by the Marquess of Hamilton (Royal Commissioner) and cast down the walls of the Episcopalian Jericho erected by James and Charles – darkly reminding potential rebuilders of the curse of Hiel the Bethelite.* Charles, determined to be obeyed, then moved the incompetent northern trained bands to the Border where, in the Bishops' Wars (1639–40), they faced a disciplined force of Covenanters under Field Marshal Alexander Leslie, who had learned his soldiering with Gustavus Adolphus. Against token opposition the Scots occupied Newcastle, cut off London's coal and demanded payment in English money thus forcing Charles, fatefully, to call the Long Parliament.

During the months that followed the Royal Prerogative was attacked at Westminster, the Scots' demands were granted and Charles came to Edinburgh in an abortive attempt to win support. He left with two important loyalties established: Archibald Campbell, 8th Earl and now 1st Marquess of Argyll, was more a Covenanter than a Royalist; James Graham, 5th Earl of Montrose, was more a Royalist than a Covenanter.

In August 1642 the Civil War broke out in England while the

Scots, the majority of whom were unsympathetic to Charles on the religious issue (and this was pre-eminently a war of conscience), looked on. In 1643 they agreed to help the Parliamentary side and, as eager to convert others as ever Charles had been, insisted in the Solemn League and Covenant of that year on the establishment of Presbyterianism in England and Ireland as an acknowledged war aim. From Marston Moor (1644) – a Parliamentary victory with Scottish aid – the tide of war in England turned against Charles until his decisive defeat at

* Joshua VI, 26; I Kings XVI, 34.

Golden Ampulla used for the
anointing of Charles I at his
Coronation in Edinburgh
on 18 June 1633

(National Museum of Antiquities of Scotland)

Naseby in 1645. Meanwhile in
Scotland Argyll's rival the
Royalist Earl (now Marquess)
of Montrose – poet-hero,
brilliant leader and unrivalled
exponent of the principles of
Long Range Penetration – had
led his column of Highland and
Irish Scots on the sparkling but
indecisive campaign of 1644–1645, through famous victories to
eventual sad defeat at Philiphaugh.

In England Charles was in poor case and saw clearly that the
reality of power now lay with Cromwell's army. This body was a
stronghold of the so-called Independents, whose highly in-
dividualistic religious tenets accorded ill with the imposition of
the uniform Presbyterianism demanded by the Scots. Seeking
therefore to drive a wedge between his opponents, Charles thought
it politic to surrender to the Scots, which he did at Newark in May
1646. But, once again, the Church problem proved intractable;
with the result that the luckless monarch was handed over to Parliament in January 1647. Later in the year Charles escaped to
Carisbrooke Castle and certain Scottish nobles were able to make
a secret "Engagement" with him, whereby he agreed to a three-
year trial of Presbyterianism in England. To support this the
(by now) 1st Duke of Hamilton marched south, only to be defeated by Cromwell at Preston (1648). Then Cromwell agreed
with Argyll that neither the Independents, nor those Scots who
opposed the "Engagement", should ever make peace with the
King. No such opportunity arose. Charles was executed at
Whitehall on 30 January 1649.

Charles II by William Dobson
(Scottish National Portrait Gallery)

Oliver Cromwell by S. Cooper
(By permission of the National Portrait Gallery, London)

CHARLES II and CROMWELL, 1649–1660

CHARLES II, 1649–1685

(Son of CHARLES I and Henrietta Maria of France)

Born 1630, was 18 when he was proclaimed King in Edinburgh, and 21 when he escaped from Worcester. He returned to Whitehall on his 30th birthday and was 54 when he died.

Married Catherine of Braganza. No legitimate issue.

Thumbnail Sketch An amorous comedian, the wide range of whose activities seldom included his duty, but *really* able.

REIGN and COMMONWEALTH

The Scots had failed in their ambition to convert England to Presbyterianism yet their connection with that country's Parliamentary Party during the Civil War left a profound and lasting impression upon their own religious life. It was the Westminster Assembly (1643–1649), attended by Scottish Commissioners from 1643 to 1647, which determined the dogmas, practice and organization which obtains in the Presbyterian Church of Scotland to this day. It is also an attractive thought that the famous metrical psalter, adopted in 1650 and generally associated with worship north of the Border, was the revision of a work by one Francis Rous, a Cornish Provost of Eton.

To do Charles I to death had been no object of the Scottish crusade. The groan which rose from the Whitehall crowd on 30 January 1649 found a ready and powerful echo in monarchical Edinburgh, while in Brussels emotion caused Montrose to faint. Within a week the Marquess of Argyll had sponsored the proclamation of Charles II as King, and soon solemn persons were crossing from Scotland to the Hague to present that humorous young man with the Covenants – documents which he found exceedingly distasteful. Rather than subscribe to them he envisaged a triumphal entry into his kingdom, with no strings attached, in the wake of a victorious Montrose. That paladin was characteristically prepared to "put it to the touch" and landed at Duncansby Head, east of John o'Groats, in April

1650. This time he led an unimpressive following recruited in Denmark and Orkney and was defeated at Carbisdale near Bonar Bridge on the 27th of the month. The first three weeks of May saw him betrayed by Neil Macleod, Laird of Assynt, condemned for treason and hanged in Edinburgh – going to his death with "sweet carriage".

Meanwhile Charles had changed his mind and decided to sign the Covenants, which cleared his way to sail into the Spey on 23 June, with the inevitable result that Cromwell marched north. The army which opposed Ironsides, under General David Leslie, suffered from the fact that the Act of Classes (1649) excluded from Scottish military service Montrose's veterans and any who had fought at Preston. But Leslie's strategy of scorched earth and avoidance of battle was already embarrassing the English when the fire-eating preachers by whom he was plagued goaded him into tactical error at Dunbar and thus to shattering defeat by Cromwell on 3 September 1650.

The Scots now withdrew to lick their wounds in the general area of Stirling, leaving the territory south of the Forth to Cromwell. Charles celebrated New Year's Day 1651 by his coronation at Scone, where the Marquess of Argyll officiated, and Leslie's recruitment improved by reason of the repeal of the Act of

Overmantel dated 1651, the initials T.U. suggest that it belonged to Sir Thomas Urquhart of Cromarty

(*National Museum of Antiquities of Scotland*)

Classes. General Lambert's victory at Inverkeithing then enabled
Cromwell to advance towards Perth while Leslie and the King
decided on the gamble of a sally into England. Cromwell turned
about, marched swiftly and caught up with them at Worcester.
Here he routed them utterly in the engagement which he called
his "crowning mercy" on 3 September. On 16 October 1651, after
a famous and perilous flight, Charles landed on the Normandy
coast.

An authoritarian English régime, backed by military force, was
now clamped upon Scotland for nine years. Law and order
reigned as never before, there was the gain of certain commercial
concessions and perhaps even a smile or two in 1653 when Sir
Thomas Urquhart of Cromarty published his translation of
Rabelais. But the Commonwealth's rule was unpopular and it
was a relief in 1660 when General Monk marched south, accompanied by the regiment which would later be distinguished as the
Coldstream Guards, to negotiate the return of the erstwhile
fugitive "Charles Stuart, a long dark man, above two yards
high".

Sir Thomas Urquhart is said to have died from laughing on hearing of the
Restoration of Charles II – a fitting end for the translator of Rabelais.

Charles II – artist unknown

(By permission of the National Portrait Gallery, London)

CHARLES II (Restored), 1660–1685

On 25 May 1660 Samuel Pepys saw Charles II land at Dover. "The shouting and joy expressed by all is past imagination," he wrote. When the news reached Edinburgh the junketing was no less enthusiastic among Scotsmen who jostled to drink, in free wine, the health of the Covenanted King whom they had crowned nine years previously.

Few Scots had been closer to Charles in 1650 than the Earl (later Duke) of Lauderdale – a characteristically able descendant of Maitland of Lethington, and a Presbyterian converted to Royalism in the 1640s. He now became Secretary to the Privy Council which once again ruled Scotland, on instructions from London, as in the days of James VI and I and Charles I.

But the bells, the cannon and the cheers of 1660 were prelude to a period of dramatic unhappiness north of the Border – which makes it well to remember that a conscientious Privy Council *was* trying to improve Scotland's economy and that Stair was writing his *Institutions of the Law of Scotland*. This great work laid the foundations of the present Scottish legal system, which differs from that of England – notably in the extent to which Roman Law has been adopted.

In January 1661 a Parliament met in Edinburgh as enthusiastically Royalist as the Cavalier Parliament which was to assemble at Westminster in May. It was swift to pass the so-called Rescissory Act, which rescinded all legislation produced since 1633, thus putting the clock back to the reign of Charles I and the days before the National Covenant of 1638. With this it was obvious that there would be ecclesiastical changes, for the restored monarch, as has been frequently quoted, reckoned that Presbyterianism was no religion for a gentleman. So Episcopacy returned and a one time Kirk minister called James Sharp concluded an obscure mission to London agreeably enough by being elevated to the archiepiscopal see of St Andrews. (He was more fortunate than the Marquess of Argyll whose London visit failed to please Charles and who came back to execution for collaboration with Cromwell.)

Restored Episcopacy did not mean repetition of Charles I's

mistaken prayer-book policy. There was no attempt to enforce Anglican practice, the services of the Kirk remained unchanged. But an organizational revival caused indignant distress among Covenanting extremists, particularly in the South-West. Since 1649 congregations had enjoyed the right of electing their own ministers. This right was now restored to local landowners, whose choice must then be ratified by the diocesan bishop. Some 300 ministers, who refused to seek this patronage and episcopal approval, forfeited their appointments. Their flocks showed a not unjustified contempt for the curates who replaced them and were soon demonstrating this by deserting the churches and worshipping under their old pastors in the field, on the hill and among the moss hags. Non-attendance at church brought fines, non-payment of fines brought dragoons and consequent discontent brought the Pentland Rising – a protest march from Dumfries to Edinburgh in 1666. The authorities, nervous of home disturbances because of the current war with Holland, reacted sharply. The withdrawing marchers were heavily hammered at Rullion Green near Penicuik by Sir Thomas Dalyell, who had learned rough ways during service in the army of the Tsar Alexis of Russia.

In 1668 Lauderdale decided courageously to take over Scotland himself, as King's Commissioner. He tried conciliation, without

out success; he resorted to force, it was a failure. Eleven miserable years culminated in the brutal murder, by Covenanters, of Archbishop Sharp and, in the same month (May 1679) the cavalry commander John Graham of Claverhouse was defeated by a well armed field congregation at Drumclog – between Kilmarnock and Strathaven. In June, however, the Covenanting army was brought to battle at Bothwell Brig, near Hamilton, and defeated by the Duke of Monmouth – Charles

Salt cellar of St Mary's College, St Andrews – about 1670
(Patrick Gairden)

(*Photographic Unit. St Salvator's College, St Andrews*)

II's natural son by Lucy Walters. The Duke's instincts were humane, and prisoners who guaranteed to keep the peace were released from their captivity in Edinburgh's Greyfriars church-yard – though some of the obdurate suffered death by execution and others by shipwreck *en route* for the West Indian plantations. The Covenanting banner, however, was immediately raised again by the fanatical Richard Cameron. He declared war on the King at the Mercat Cross of Sanquhar, and was killed by dragoons at Aird's Moss, 18 miles east of Ayr, shortly thereafter (1680). In 1681 the Duke of York, Charles's brother, became Commissioner, and severity increased. When Charles lay dying in Whitehall in February 1685, what has been called "The Killing Time" was beginning in Scotland – but the King had not seen that country since 1651.

James VII and II by Sir Peter Lely

(*Scottish National Portrait Gallery*)

JAMES VII and II, 1685–1688

(Son of CHARLES I and Henrietta Maria, brother of CHARLES II)

Born 1633, was 51 when he ascended the throne, and 55 when he fled the country.

Married Anne Hyde – had 8 children including:
> MARY, who married William of Orange – WILLIAM III
> ANNE

Married Mary of Modena – had 7 children including:
> Prince James Francis Edward, (to the Jacobites: JAMES VIII and III, to the Hanoverians: "The Old Pretender").

Thumbnail Sketch   A serious and courageous professional soldier, unattractively sensual, the worst of the Stuarts at managing his subjects.

THE REIGN

The fact that James was a Roman Catholic had been common knowledge since 1673, when he had resigned his position as Lord High Admiral of England in accordance with the Test Act which restricted crown offices to Anglican communicants. The zeal of the Royal convert was evidenced by a bigotry which Charles II, himself not remarkable for religious enthusiasm, called *la sottise de mon frère* – a foolishness which would eventually lose James his throne. Attempts were made by supporters of the Exclusion Bill (1680–1681) to prevent his ever becoming King, but this endeavour failed and his succession passed off smoothly enough in England and in Scotland.

In a matter of months, however, there were rebellions in both kingdoms, with the object of putting the Duke of Monmouth on the throne. In the North the 9th Earl of Argyll was leader. He had been in trouble previously both with the Commonwealth authorities and the Stuarts and had saved himself in 1681 by a romantic escape from Edinburgh castle when under sentence of death for treason. He now returned from the continent to his own country, failed dismally to stimulate a rising, was captured, and decapitated on 29 June 1685 by a guillotine called "The Maiden"* – the very machine which had despatched his father in 1661. A week later Monmouth himself was defeated at Sedgemoor and was executed by the barbarous Jack Ketch on 15 July.

A number of Covenanters, already under arrest, suffered at this juncture. As Argyll made his futile effort in the West, so these potentially subversive prisoners were moved east, where all suffered and some died in the so-called "Whigs' Vault" at the great castle of Dunnottar near Stonehaven. (The name "Whig" – with its connotations of cattle thieving – was now used contemptuously to denote these Presbyterian extremists.) Meanwhile a Covenanting zealot called James Renwick, who would not assist Argyll's rebellion because he doubted the Earl's religious orthodoxy, had joined the Cameronians – the followers of the late Richard Cameron (see page 167). Renwick denounced James VII and II with Old Testament ferocity in a second Sanquhar Declaration, and the Government's anti-covenanting campaign was stepped up. Once again "that dour deevil" John Graham of Claverhouse swept through the South-West seeking whom he might devour in the way of rebels, and the notorious "Killing

ENTRANCE TO DUNNOTTAR

Time" was in full swing. Many memorials perpetuate the saga of the Covenanters, as the defenders of Civil and Religious Liberty, and it is certain that atrocities were committed in the name of government at this time. Yet the faults were not all on one side and the Covenanters displayed a provocative confidence in their own righteousness and in the ultimate fate of their enemies:

"They'll know at Resurrection Day
    To murder saints was no sweet play"

– so runs an inscription in the cathedral of kindly St Mungo in

* Now in the National Museum of Antiquities of Scotland in Edinburgh.

The Holyrood Monstrance (1686) for the Chapel Royal in
Edinburgh

*(National Museum of Antiquities of Scotland – on loan from the Reverend Mother
Superior, St Margaret's Convent, Edinburgh)*

Glasgow. The fact is that *neither* side believed in toleration.

So James's Declarations and Letters of Indulgence (1687–
1688), giving freedom of worship to Romanists and Dissenters,
cut as little ice in Scotland as they did in England. They were
accompanied by the promotion of the King's co-religionists to
high places in both countries, and were recognized as a step
towards the Royal religious object – the restoration of Roman
Catholicism. The birth of a son to the King and Mary of Modena
on 10 June 1688 conjured up a picture of perpetuation of this
policy – and soon powerful persons in England were in corres-
pondence with William of Orange, James's nephew and son-in-
law, inviting him to undertake an invasion and overthrow the
King. In November William landed at Torbay and James, dis-
couraged by defection and desertion, fled. He was captured, but
sensibly permitted to escape, which enabled him to join his
Queen and son in France as the year 1688 drew to its close.

William III after Kneller
(*Scottish National Portrait Gallery*)

Mary – engraving by Blooteling after Lely
(*Scottish National Portrait Gallery*)

WILLIAM and MARY, 1689–1694

WILLIAM III, 1694–1702

(WILLIAM was the son of William II of Orange and Mary, daughter of CHARLES I. MARY was the eldest daughter of JAMES VII and II and Anne Hyde)

WILLIAM, born 1650, was 38 when he ascended the throne, and 51 when he died. MARY, born 1662, was 26 when she ascended the throne, and 32 when she died.

WILLIAM and MARY had no issue.

Thumbnail Sketch (WILLIAM) A cold unattractive man, a second-rate soldier of immense tenacity, an able diplomat and architect of alliances.

THE REIGN

On 13 February 1689 a Convention offered England's crown to William and Mary as joint sovereigns. A similar body in Scotland followed suit on 11 April. In the southern kingdom the "Glorious Revolution" was over. In the North there were troubles to come.

James VII and II had failed, but the Stuart dynasty was now 318 years old and commanded formidable Scottish loyalties, particularly in the Highlands. Thus Jacobitism was born and found its first leader in John Graham of Claverhouse, created Viscount Dundee by James in November 1688. By the next summer Dundee was commanding a force of Highlanders, ready to fight for the monarch who had fled, and eager to pull down the great Campbell clan which supported William. Under this brilliant leader, and on carefully chosen ground near Pitlochry, the Highlanders surprised government troops commanded by General Mackay. In this battle of Killiecrankie (27 July 1689) the Highland charge hit and routed Mackay's men as they were fixing their plug bayonets into their musket muzzles – but Dundee was killed. Nevertheless a number of Highlanders pressed on to Dunkeld where a newly raised regiment awaited them. The authorities had turned to Claverhouse's old Covenanting opponents, the followers of Richard Cameron and James Renwick, for recruits. At Dunkeld, whence the Jacobites were forced to withdraw discomfited, the unit which was later to win distinction as the Cameronians or Scottish Rifles originally showed its mettle.

Religion in Scotland was one of the first problems which faced the new régime. It was clear that episcopacy, restored in 1661, must go, and so back came the Westminster Confession, brain-child of the Westminster Assembly of 1643–1649 (see page 161), with congregations once again choosing their own ministers, and full Presbyterian organization, which has continued to this day.

But the major factor in British history during the period 1689–1702 was, of course, Dutch William's preoccupation with his wars against Louis XIV. The Sun King naturally supported the exiled Stuarts and French troops assisted James in Ireland, whom William defeated at the battle of the Boyne (1 July 1690). The government feared similar trouble in Scotland, where the Jacobite, anti-Campbell, element represented a potential Highland Fifth Column. Eventually the Chiefs were ordered to swear allegiance to William before 1 January 1692. The story of how McIan, chief of the Macdonalds of Glencoe, failed to achieve this before 6 January is well known. The Master of Stair, Secretary of State for Scotland and son of the famous lawyer (see page 165), decided to punish this ancient cattle thief by an exemplary

atrocity. A bungled operation by a detachment of the Earl of Argyll's Regiment of Foot (a Campbell unit), ordered to slaughter all inhabitants of Glencoe under seventy, resulted in thirty-eight Macdonald casualties on 13 February 1692. The action is insignificant compared with the standard set by the twentieth century, but the manner of it, and the fact that the troops had accepted the hospitality of their victims, brought William's government into disrepute in Scotland.

Silver mounted Quaich (drinking cup) central boss engraved
with crown and J.R.7 – dated 1692 (clearly a Jacobite object)
(*National Museum of Antiquities of Scotland*)

Nor was the Darien affair of 1698–1700 calculated to enhance
the popularity of this administration. Scotland, much the poorer
of the partners under the Dual Monarchy, was an envious spec-
tator of England's treasure by foreign trade, being herself excluded from this by England's Navigation Acts and the monopolies of the East India Company and the Africa Company. The
Scots thus accepted with enthusiasm the plan of a Dumfriesshire
economist and founder of the Bank of England, William Paterson,
who prophesied untold wealth from a settlement on the Gulf of
Darien (Panama) where the Atlantic and the Pacific are a mere
forty miles apart. A company was founded for this purpose, with
the full blessing of the Scottish Parliament, backed by patriotic
fervour and heavy national investment. Initially English and
foreign speculators showed interest, but commercial jealousies
and William III's determination to retain the friendship of
Spain, in whose sphere of influence Darien lay, led to the withdrawal of financial support and active opposition from the English
government and its colonies. The Scots, however, pressed on,
mounted two expeditions to Darien, and, between July 1698 and
April 1700, lost two thousand lives and a minimum of £200,000
as the result of tropical disease and Spanish action.

On 20 February 1702 a Hampton Court molehill threw William's horse, the King broke his collar-bone, pleurisy followed
and, on 8 March, he died. There were plenty in Scotland who
toasted the "little gentleman in velvet" whose subterranean
activities had caused the monarch's death.

Queen Anne by William Wissing

(*Scottish National Portrait Gallery*)

ANNE, 1702–1714

(Daughter of JAMES VII and II and Anne Hyde. Sister of MARY)

Born 1665, was 37 when she ascended the throne, and 49 when she died.

Married Prince George of Denmark – had seventeen children, most of whom died in infancy and all of whom predeceased her, including:

William, Duke of Gloucester

Thumbnail Sketch   Religious, virtuous, kindly, dull and a prey to ill-health. Not, as has sometimes been suggested, a crypto-Jacobite.

THE REIGN

Nothing had happened since 1660 to make the centenary of the Dual Monarchy in 1703 an occasion for thanksgiving in Scotland. Under absentee monarchs the country, already to some extent embittered during the Covenanting troubles, had been recently plagued by bad harvests and rendered indignant by the English government's behaviour over Glencoe and Darien. The reign of Queen Anne opened in an atmosphere of economic and psychological depression.

In England in 1700 the death of Anne's heir, the eleven-year-old William, Duke of Gloucester, had caused anxiety about the succession. The Act of Settlement (1701) laid down that in the likely event of this Princess's dying childless, the crown should then pass to the Electress Sophia of Hanover (granddaughter of James VI and I, see page 145) and "the heirs of her body being Protestants". The Scots were not consulted over this arrangement and many of them were delighted when, on the death of James VII and II (September 1701), Louis XIV recognized his son, Prince James Francis Edward, as James VIII and III. By May 1702 England and France were locked in the War of the Spanish Succession (which would last until 1713) and the idea of a disgruntled Scotland welcoming a King from over the water, eager to deliver a stab in the back with French support, was a possibility which caused uneasiness in Whitehall.

Each country, then, had a major problem. With Scotland it was primarily a question of economics – the desire for foreign trade. With England it was, above all, a matter of strategy – the security of the northern flank. In both cases a solution was to be found in Union, with which William III had been preoccupied as his life ebbed away, but relations had to deteriorate even further before that Union became possible.

Indignation at England's bland assumption that the Scots would accept the Act of Settlement, unconsulted, moved Parliament in Edinburgh to retaliate with the Act of Security of 1704 – the year of Blenheim. It was laid down that twenty days should pass after Anne's death before any choice of her successor would be made in Scotland and that Protestantism and Stuart blood were essential qualifications for the appointment. The Electress of Hanover would not be selected unless freedom of trade, religion and government were guaranteed to the northern kingdom.

This essentially separatist enactment might have precipitated Civil War. England's reply was far from conciliatory and took the form of the Aliens Act, demanding the Scots' agreement, by Christmas 1705, to the accession of Sophia, on pain of their incurring the disabilities of aliens with, in addition, the stoppage of all trade between the two countries. A bad situation became

Gesso Panel from Inchbraoch House, Montrose – Royal
visit to the Fleet about 1708

(National Museum of Antiquities of Scotland)

intolerable in April 1705, when an English merchant-captain
named Green was hanged at Leith with two of his officers for
alleged piracy against a Scottish ship, of which crime all three
were utterly and obviously innocent.

But finally sense prevailed. As the guns boomed at Ramillies in
May 1706, thirty-one Scottish and thirty-one English commissioners were considering common problems at Whitehall. In a
time of crisis they accomplished their mission with political
acumen and business-like despatch. After long debate, accompanied by riots, their proposed Act of Union was accepted by
Scotland's parliament. It had a smooth passage at Westminster
and became law on 1 May 1707 – a great watershed date in the
history of the British Isles.

First and foremost the Parliaments of the two countries were
merged, Scotland adding 45 members to a House of Commons of
512 and 16 peers to a House of Lords whose strength had been
190. She gained the long-coveted equality of opportunity with
England over matters of foreign trade, and conceded agreement
to England's decision about the Electress Sophia. The two countries accepted a common system of coinage, weights and measures,
but retained their own laws, courts and church settlements.
Finally Scotland received compensation for sharing responsibility

for the English national debt and for her own losses over the Darien affair.

But there was no prosperous Scottish transformation scene – men had to await the slow passage of fifty years for that. Meanwhile the Kirk grumbled at the return of landowners' patronage and the toleration of Episcopalians – Union, in fact, brought increased discontent. In 1708 a French expedition failed to land Prince James Francis Edward, the Chevalier de St Georges, at Burntisland. That, at least, was a mercy.

THE IMPACT OF UNION
1707–1820

(Anne	1702–1714)
George I	1714–1727
George II	1727–1760
George III	1760–1820

In France

Louis XIV	1643–1715
Louis XV	1715–1774
Louis XVI	1774–1792
First Republic	1792–1804
Napoleon I	1804–1814
Louis XVIII	1814–1824

Culzean Castle 1777–1792 by Robert Adam
A feature of the castle is the flat reserved for General
Eisenhower during his lifetime
(Reproduced by permission of the National Trust for Scotland)

THE IMPACT OF UNION
1707–1820

The appeal of the Jacobite risings may stir you as you pass through Braemar (1715), by Eilean Donan Castle and Glen Shiel (1719), and you must not miss Glenfinnan (1745) or Culloden (1746) with their admirable historical expositions of Prince Charles Edward's adventure. By which token you may also be interested in "Hanoverian" military installations, built to combat this menace, such as Ruthven Barracks near Kingussie, and Fort George, north-east of Inverness.

This is also a period of distinguished architects and civil engineers. William Adam and his sons, James Craig and Robert Mylne, were among those at work on houses, castles and churches, while Thomas Telford and John Rennie were designing canals, bridges and harbours. Houses of particular interest are Mellerstain near Kelso, Hopetoun near Edinburgh and Duff House at Banff; Culzean (on the Ayr–Girvan road) and Inveraray are Georgian castles enlivened by a dash of romantic Gothic. There are a number of good eighteenth-century churches, among which special mention may be made of St Andrew's, Glasgow.

The largest area of Georgian planning and architecture in any city is to be seen in Craig's New Town of Edinburgh (1767–1800) and there are many notable examples of planned towns and villages (one of the social phenomena of the period) such as Gifford, Inveraray, Tomintoul, Grantown-on-Spey, Fochabers and Ullapool. Meanwhile go on looking at roads and bridges and inspect, at least, the Caledonian Canal.

Finally you should certainly combine two literary pilgrimages with your sight-seeing: the Burns sites in the South-West (the family cottage at Alloway, the Bachelors Club at Tarbolton and Souter Johnnie's cottage at Kirkoswald) are all within easy reach of Ayr, and remember that in 1781 this genius, whom Goethe regarded as the first of lyric poets, was made a burger of Dumfries, where he died ten years later. And, of course, go to the great house at Abbotsford, near Melrose, where Sir Walter Scott lived from 1812 to 1832.

Prince James Francis Edward by François de Troy

(Scottish National Portrait Gallery)

Son of James VII and II and Mary of Modena. Born 1688. Married Clementina
Sobieska. Had two sons: Prince Charles Edward and Prince Henry Benedict.
Died 1766.

George I, bust by Michael Rysbrack

(By permission of the Governing Body of Christ Church, Oxford)

GEORGE I, 1714–1727

(Son of Ernest Augustus, Elector of Brunswick-Lüneburg – (or Hanover) – and Sophia, granddaughter of JAMES VI and I. Great-grandson of JAMES VI and I)

Born 1660, was 54 when he ascended the throne, and 67 when he died.

Married Sophia Dorothea of Celle (whom he divorced in 1694). Had two children:
GEORGE II.
Sophia Dorothea – married Frederick William I of Prussia.

Thumbnail Sketch A very unattractive German who disliked Britain, but possessed the virtue of courage.

THE REIGN

On 8 June 1714 Sophia of Hanover died at Herrnhausen, pre-deceasing Queen Anne by some two months. So the crown passed, in accordance with the Act of Settlement (see page 145), to the Electress's eldest son "the high and mighty Prince George, Elector of Brunswick-Lüneburg", of whom the Jacobites sang:

> "Wha the deil hae we gotten for a king,
> But a wee wee German lairdie?"

Indeed it seemed that this might be a golden opportunity for a come-back by Prince James Francis Edward. Jacobite feeling in many districts of the Highlands remained strong and there were also plenty of Lowlanders who had little use for "the sad and sorrowfu' Union" which appeared to have brought nothing but continued poverty and new taxes. So James gave orders for his standard to be raised in Scotland by the Earl of Mar, whose pro-testations of loyalty to William III, Anne and George I had not prevented a close relationship with the Stuart exiles of St Germain and Bar-le-Duc, and whose erratic policy of alternately support-ing and opposing the Union had earned him the nickname of "Bobbing John". When, on 6 September 1715, the golden ball which crowned Mar's flagstaff at Braemar toppled off, there were superstitious murmurings. However some 10,000 supporters soon gathered, considerably outnumbering the government troops north of the Border. What followed was inglorious. Mar, a highly amateur soldier, captured Perth – and remained there in indecision. Eventually one of his lieutenants, Brigadier Mackintosh of Borlum, crossed the Forth with a small force and moved to join the Scottish and English Jacobites of the western Border country. Their southward advance ended in defeat at "Proud Preston in Lancashire" while, on the very same day (13 November 1715), Mar confronted the Duke of Argyll at Sheriffmuir, north-east of Stirling, where:

> "There's some say that we wan,
>   Some say that they wan,
>   Some say that nane wan at a' man",

but the fruits of victory fell to Argyll. James landed at Peterhead in December, but left Montrose for France, with Mar, on 4 February 1716. His observation "for me it is no new thing to be unfortunate" was hardly a rallying cry, his melancholy bearing lowered morale, and his impolitic, if high-minded, determination not to renounce Roman Catholicism blighted his chances.

By eighteenth-century standards the rebels of the Fifteen were mildly treated. Two of the Preston prisoners – the popular young English Earl of Derwentwater and the Scottish Viscount Kenmure

– suffered on Tower Hill, nineteen noble gentlemen lost their peerages, a number of persons of low degree were shipped overseas, and an ineffective effort was made to disarm the clans. But the Jacobites returned to the charge in 1719. The Spanish first minister Alberoni, bitter opponent of the Treaty of Utrecht, by which Spain had ceded Minorca and Gibraltar to Great Britain, sent an expedition against England to assist a rising in Scotland. The Scottish venture

Figure of a Highland Gentleman,
French – about 1715
(*National Museum of Antiquities of Scotland*)

was led by George Keith, 10th Earl Marischal (later favourite of
Frederick the Great) with 300 Spanish soldiers under command.
Foul weather prevented any ships reaching England, but Keith
landed in Loch Alsh, occupied Eilean Donan Castle and was
defeated in Glen Shiel. His troops surrendered and he escaped.
A determined and scientific effort was now made by the government to put a stop to these rebellions. A further Disarming Act
was passed in 1725 (but the clans persisted in the practice of
only surrendering non-battleworthy weapons), while General
George Wade started on his immortal Highland communications
enterprise (1724–1734) remembered in the familiar jingle:

"Had you seen these roads before they were made,
You would lift up your hands and bless General Wade."

By 1727, when the reign ended, Scotland remained poor, and
serious anti-taxation riots showed that the Union was still unpopular. Nevertheless the Education Act of 1696 (each parish to
have a school) was beginning to take effect, Allan Ramsay had
written *The Gentle Shepherd*, Daniel Defoe had been impressed by
the cleanliness and beauty of Glasgow – already importing an impressive tonnage of tobacco, and the Society for Improving in the
Knowledge of Agriculture brought promise of better things to
come.

George II by John Shackleton

(*Scottish National Portrait Gallery*)

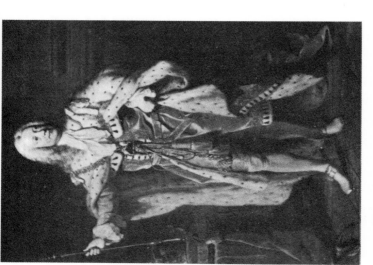

Prince Charles Edward by Antonio David

(*Scottish National Portrait Gallery*)

Son of Prince James Francis Edward and Clementina Sobieska. Born 1720.
Married Louisa of Stolberg. No legitimate issue. Died 1788.

GEORGE II, 1727–1760

(Son of GEORGE I and Sophia Dorothea of Celle)

Born 1683, was 44 when he ascended the throne, and 77 when he died.

Married Caroline of Ansbach – had eight children including:
  Frederick, Prince of Wales (father of GEORGE III).
  William Augustus, Duke of Cumberland.

Thumbnail Sketch   A limited but courageous character. The last British monarch to command his army in the field (Dettingen 1743). The patron of Handel.

THE REIGN

About a quarter of a century was to elapse before the promise of better things, observable at the end of the reign of George I, could be seen to be in process of fulfilment. In 1727 wide areas of Scotland were totally unaffected by the agricultural studies which led to the rotation of crops and the introduction of potatoes and turnips, clover and cabbage. In general poverty-stricken peasants cultivated poor land by primitive methods, leading a miserable existence from which recurrent small-pox epidemics frequently provided a merciful release.

Nor was there yet any marked growth in the popularity of the Union – even in 1740, when the Roxburghshire poet James Thomson (in the comfort of Surrey) was moved to write *Rule, Britannia*, few Scots could share his ex-patriate enthusiasm. Readers of *The Heart of Midlothian* will recollect that public opinion north of the Border admired the adventurers who profitably evaded the Whitehall government's customs duties. When Captain John Porteous, of Edinburgh's City Guard, fired on an unruly crowd at the hanging of a popular smuggler, he was condemned to death. A subsequent stay of execution aroused indignation in the Scottish capital and led to the famous Porteous Riot of 1737 in which a highly organized mob extracted this over-zealous officer from the Tolbooth and subjected him to their own rough justice on the traditional Grassmarket site.

But the most dramatic event of the reign was the Jacobite

Rising of 1745 – an embarrassment in view of Britain's involvement in the War of the Austrian Succession (1742–1748). On 3 August Prince Charles Edward (aged 25), son of "James VIII and III" (who knew nothing of the project), appeared off Eriskay, between South Uist and Barra, and then made a landing in Moidart with seven companions. His reception was lukewarm but his personality triumphed, the Macdonalds and Camerons agreed to back him, and on 19 August his standard was raised at lovely Glenfinnan on the "Road to the Isles" where others rallied "to proclaim his daddie". A month later James III was similarly proclaimed in Edinburgh, which soon gleamed with White Cockades and White Roses, while Holyroodhouse resounded with the music of the pipes and the tap of dancing feet. General Sir John Cope was defeated at Prestonpans and early in November the Prince moved south for London. Though English Jacobite support was negligible, London panicked. Nevertheless, upon reaching Derby, the Prince was reluctantly persuaded to turn back. Withdrawing to Scotland he inflicted a profitless defeat on General Hawley at Falkirk, and eventually reached Inverness, where he paused to reorganize his army of some 5,000 men. Government troops, 9,000 strong, under William Augustus, Duke of Cumberland, 25-year-old son of George II, advanced to meet him. This methodical commander, who had taught his men a drill

to meet the Highland charge, defeated his "cousin Charles" in wind and sleet on Drummossie Moor near Culloden House on 16 April 1746. The Young Chevalier was on the run for five months before he could sail for France. The sum of £30,000 was on his head, but Flora Macdonald typified the courage which kept Prince Charlie's secret and the fact that no "fause Menteith" or Laird of Assynt crossed his path saved him from the fate of Wallace and Montrose.

Tortoise-shell Snuff-box with portrait of Prince James Francis
Edward. "A gift from Prince Charles Stewart to Miss Flora
Macdonald 1746"

(National Museum of Antiquities of Scotland)

The immediate aftermath of Culloden was grim. The wounded
were butchered, the "Sidier Roy" (red soldiers) carried fire and
sword into the Highlands, there were 120 executions, 700 deaths in
prison and over 1,000 transportations. Disarmament, this time,
was thorough. For some forty years the pipes were silent, the
tartan was proscribed and many estates were confiscated. Above
all the fact that the chief was no longer allowed to exercise
military or judicial authority over his people meant that from
having been a patriarch he became a landlord and that, as far as
the clans were concerned, the old order passed. In honour of these
events Handel greeted Cumberland's return to London with *See
the Conquering Hero Comes*!

But the Scottish picture did not remain uniformly black. Before
1760 there had been great intellectual, literary, scientific and
artistic activity. Among distinguished names those of the philosopher David Hume, the historian William Robertson, the political
economist Adam Smith, the surgeon Alexander Monro, the
physician Joseph Black and the Adam family of architects stand
out. In addition agriculture was at last improving, turnpike roads
were replacing ancient tracks, the Glasgow tobacco trade boomed
and, in the year of the King's death, the Carron Iron Works
opened.

George III by Allan Ramsay

(Reproduced by permission of the Trustees of the Wallace Collection)

Prince Charles Edward
attributed to H. D. Hamilton

(Scottish National Portrait Gallery)

Prince Henry Benedict by
Antonio David

(Scottish National Portrait Gallery)
Son of Prince James Francis Edward
and Clementina Sobieska. Born 1725.
Priest of the Roman Church. Cardinal York 1747. No issue. Died 1807.

GEORGE III, 1760–1820

(Son of Frederick, Prince of Wales, and Augusta of Saxe-
Gotha. Grandson of GEORGE II)

Born 1738, was 22 when he ascended the throne, and 81 when he died.

Married Charlotte of Mecklenburg-Strelitz – had fifteen children including:

GEORGE IV	Ernest, Duke of Cumberland
Frederick, Duke of York	(King of Hanover, 1837–1857)
WILLIAM IV	Augustus, Duke of Sussex
Edward, Duke of Kent	Adolphus, Duke of Cambridge

Thumbnail Sketch A lover of England whose personal impact upon Scotland was negligible. He pensioned the last Stuart claimant.

THE REIGN

George III may have "gloried in the name of Britain", but he never visited Scotland, which underwent an astonishing transformation during his reign. A remarkable feature of these sixty years was the intellectual upsurge which led Matthew Bramble, in Smollett's *Humphry Clinker*, to call Edinburgh "a hot-bed of genius" – and it is indeed impossible to mention here all the names which made up this galaxy of ability in later Georgian Scotland. Dr Johnson enjoyed the company of William Robertson, the historian, Adam Ferguson, the philosopher, and James Gregory, Edinburgh's Professor of Medicine, when Boswell introduced him to them in 1773. He also rightly dismissed as an imposture James Macpherson's alleged translations of the work of a second-century Gaelic poet, "the so-called Ossian", which Goethe carried in his pocket at Wetzlar and Bonaparte took to Egypt. Edinburgh at this time was indeed the Athens of the North, where houses built by the Adam family held pictures painted by Allan Ramsay, the younger, the Nasmyths and Raeburn. The period culminated in the greatness of Robert Burns and Walter Scott.

Such a flowering suggests educational facilities of the kind which normally accompany prosperity. In fact neither the ideal of

Knox nor that of the 1696 act had yet been realized, but Scotland
was richer in schools than many other countries and enjoyed
universities offering high standards for low fees. And there had
been an enormous advance in wealth. Glasgow's prosperity has
already been mentioned and even before 1773, when the deepen-
ing of the Clyde was started, this city was importing more than
half the tobacco shipped to Britain. When the American Revolution stopped this, in came rum and sugar from the Caribbean.
Nor were Scotsmen living by trade alone. During the latter half
of the eighteenth century an agricultural revolution was accomplished by improving landlords, which transformed the Lowlands
and brought Englishmen north, not to teach but to learn. Less
attractive, but even more profitable, were the changes accomplished by the Industrial Revolution. A series of inventions,
starting with Kay's flying shuttle in 1733, moved the textile
industry from the cottage to the factory, linen manufacture
eventually dropped to second place, cotton became king and the
whole received tremendous impetus from work on the steam-
engine by James Watt of Greenock. This vastly increased the importance of coal, the iron industry developed apace, and there

was a heavy and insalubrious
concentration of population in the
western part of the Central Lowlands. All this stimulated the development of communications. It
was an age of canals, bridges,
harbours and roads – of Telford,
Rennie and McAdam "whose
name" (so runs his memorial at
Carsphairn) "is enshrined in every
language and perpetuated in every
land".

The Highlands did not share the
new wealth or the new opportunities for employment that became
available in the Lowlands. In the
course of this reign the post-Forty-
Five type of Chief appreciated

the profits of sheep-farming and, not for the first time in Britain's history, small men had to make way for animals. The so-called "Highland Clearances", carried out at best with imagination, at worst with inhumanity, forced some to wring a living from coastal crofts, others to move to the new industrial areas, and many to emigrate. The British Army recruited the Highland Regiments whose formidable roll of battle honours, before 1820, records service as far east as Assaye, as far south as the Cape of Good Hope, as far west as North America, on the famous battlefields of the Peninsula and at Waterloo.

The American and French Revolutions awakened Scotland from a certain degree of political lethargy, and the 1780s and 1790s saw the beginnings of agitation for reform both in burgh administration and in the franchise. However Henry Dundas, first Viscount Melville, who held office at Westminster on and off from 1782 to 1805, succeeded in managing Scottish representation in the Tory interest. The early enthusiasm of Scotsmen for the events in France was damped down in 1793, when Britain went

to war with the young republic and was subsequently subjected
to repressive anti-Jacobin legislation. The years after Waterloo,
when a victorious Britain suffered unemployment and hunger,
saw a recrudescence of unrest. England had her "Peterloo"
(1819), Scotland her "Radical War" (1820) when Glasgow disturbances culminated in a skirmish between weavers and cavalry
at Bonnymuir. Soon both countries would be clamouring for
Parliamentary Reform.

THE TRANSFORMATION OF
SCOTLAND

Reform and Politics
The Royal Family in Scotland
The Condition of Scotland
"The Spirit of Rambling and Adventure"
Godliness, Good Learning and Kindred Subjects

The Forth Railway Bridge
(Photograph by courtesy of the Scottish Tourist Board)

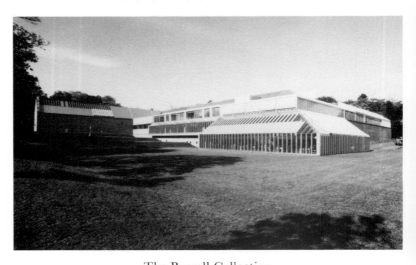

The Burrell Collection
*(Photograph by courtesy of The Burrell Collection,
Glasgow Art Gallery & Museum)*

"No municipality has ever received from one of its native sons a gift of such munificence as that which, in 1944, the city of Glasgow accepted from Sir William and Lady Burrell."

(The Burrell Collection, John Julius Norwich)

THE TRANSFORMATION OF SCOTLAND
1820–1985

The Victorian Era and the twentieth century offer a bewildering variety of "sights". The grim conditions of the Industrial Revolution, whose relics are now classified as "Industrial Archaeology", not unnaturally stimulated escapist revivals. In Glasgow one finds Neo-Classical houses built by Alexander Thomson (famous as "Greek" Thomson), Neo-Gothic churches and also sound, functional, opulent Victorian dwellings, which serve as a monument to the go-getting commercial prosperity of the period. And there are the remarkable pinnacles of Marischal College, Aberdeen, the turrets of Donaldson's Hospital, Edinburgh – none of which are so satisfying as that great feat of engineering, the Forth Railway Bridge of 1890. In the country observe the Neo-Baronial of Ayton Castle, near Berwick, of Balmoral and of many other Scottish stately homes. And let it not be forgotten that this is also a period of gardens and garden revival, making special mention of those of Drummond Castle, near Muthill, south of Crieff (1840), Lochinch Castle, near Stranraer (mid-nineteenth century) and Inverewe, north-east of Gairloch (1862).

As the nineteenth century faded into the twentieth – with its unparalleled architectural opportunities owing to technical advance, efficient transport and wide variety of material – the great Charles Rennie Mackintosh was at work on the Glasgow School of Art (1897–1909) and Hill House at Helensburgh, forming a link between the Victorians and the Moderns. The inter-war years saw the Scottish National War Memorial in Edinburgh (Neo-Gothic still, but on no account to be missed), and, also in the capital, St Andrew's House, Calton Hill – essentially representative of its time. As well as hydro-electric installations, nuclear reactors and the Forth Road Bridge of 1964, you may also find interest in Scotland's post-1945 "New Towns". But perhaps there is greater pleasure in the rehabilitation of her small burghs and villages – Lauder, Inveraray in the West, the little harbours of Fife (Pittenweem, Crail, etc.), Banff and Portsoy in the North-East.

W. E. Gladstone by F. von Lenbach
(Scottish National Portrait Gallery)

Scottish Prime Ministers: W. E. Gladstone, four times Prime Minister between
1868 and 1894. Lord Rosebery 1894–1895, Lord Balfour 1902–1905, Sir
Henry Campbell-Bannerman 1905–1908, Andrew Bonar-Law 1922–1923,
James Ramsay Macdonald 1924, 1929–1935

THE TRANSFORMATION OF SCOTLAND

From the Death of George III to 1985

REFORM AND POLITICS

In the year 1830 reform was in the air. George IV died, the reactionary Charles X was driven from Paris and replaced by Louis Philippe, Belgium declared herself independent of Holland, there were liberal stirrings throughout Europe from Spain to Poland. In England, after the General Election of 1830, the Duke of Wellington, as Premier, declared: "The legislation and system of representation possesses the full and entire confidence of the country" – a sensational observation which led to his resignation and replacement by the Whig Lord Grey.

In fact forward-thinking minds had been exercised for years by the anomalies of the ridiculous system which governed Great Britain's parliamentary elections and distribution of seats. We are familiar with England's "Pocket-Boroughs" and "Rotten Boroughs" – the situation in Scotland was every bit as absurd. That country's population numbered one million souls in 1801 and two million six hundred thousand in 1841. It will be recalled that in 1707 she had acquired the privilege of sending forty-five members to the House of Commons at Westminster. Fifteen of these were returned by the sixty-six royal burghs – insolvent anachronisms whose deeply entrenched oligarchical councils enjoyed the profits of municipal peculation and the privilege of manipulating an extremely complicated electoral procedure. The remaining thirty members were the choice of some three thousand county electors who qualified for the franchise by reason of holding land direct from the crown.

The passing of Lord Grey's great Reform Bill was watched with enthusiastic interest in Edinburgh. It became law in June 1832 and was followed by the Scottish Act a month later. The two measures were, naturally, similar. There was a rational redistribution of seats, Scotland (with eight new burghs) now had fifty-three members in the House of Commons, the vote was to be exercised in the burghs by householders paying £10 annual rent, in the counties by those who owned land worth £10 a year or who paid £50 on an annual lease. Both north and south of the Tweed the aristocratic landowners had gone into partnership with the middle class.

After the Reform Acts of 1867–1868 and 1884–1885 pretty well every householder enjoyed the vote (with the blessing of a secret ballot after 1872). In the twentieth century Great Britain has seen universal suffrage, first for men and subsequently for women. Today, with a population of approximately 5,200,000, Scotland is represented by seventy-two members at Westminster.

Parliamentary Reform was, naturally, followed by reforms in local government while, politically, Scotland settled down to a long period during which the Liberals (late Whigs) replaced the Conservatives (late Tories) as the dominant party in the country. After 1850 Trade Unionism made great advances and, with the rise of Socialism, the 1880s and 1890s saw the emergence of the Labour Party in Scotland – the creation of R. B. Cunningham-Graham and James Keir-Hardie, who became Secretary of the Scottish Miners' Federation in 1892. With this, Nationalist demands began to make themselves heard, which were by no means wholly met by the creation of the office of Secretary for Scotland in 1885. By the time that this appointment had been elevated to that of Secretary of State in the 1920s, the Labour Party had made great progress and the Scottish National Party, demanding a Scottish Parliament, was coming into being. It was the outbreak of war in 1939 which temporarily quietened Nationalist clamour, rather than the move, in the same year, of a large part of the Scottish Office (bringing with it the Scottish departments for Home Affairs, Agriculture and Fisheries, Health and Education) from London to St Andrew's House on Edinburgh's Calton Hill. By 1948 the Nationalists were on the move again and produced a document with the evocative title of the Scottish Covenant which revived the agitation for a Scottish Parliament. In 1967 the coal-mining centre of Hamilton returned the National Party's second representative to Westminster, though by then the country was maintaining a reasonably even balance between Conservatives and Labour.

In a Great Britain bedevilled by discontents, which must be expected when a once mighty imperial power gropes her way into an uncertain future, Scotland is not alone in feeling disenchantment and frustration. It is not surprising that, north of the Border, this should sometimes take the form of a desire to break away from London. Enthusiasm varies with the years. The 1979 referendum gave Scots the chance of a greater degree of independence from Westminster but, while more people voted for devolution (the delegation of power) than against it, the number of "yes" voters was too low to reach the quota required by parliament. Many people thought it quite wrong that the issue should be decided in this way, with those who failed to vote counting, in effect, as "no" voters. But for all that, many, while respecting and supporting measures in sympathy with Scottish national feeling, will not endorse complete separatism – a concept which disregards the powerful economic and cultural bonds which, happily, hold the peoples of Great Britain naturally together.

THE ROYAL FAMILY IN SCOTLAND

When George IV decided upon a journey to Edinburgh in 1822 a great opportunity presented itself. Charles I had been crowned there in 1633, Charles II had ventured into his northern kingdom during a few months in 1650 and 1651, but the only subsequent Royal Progress – the unwelcome one of William Augustus, Duke of Cumberland, in 1746 – had left Scotland with the bitter memories of Culloden and its aftermath. It was the opinion of Sir Walter Scott that, if George IV played his part well during his stay, he might strike a blow for Scottish reconciliation with the House of Hanover, for the popularity of the Union and also for the national self-consciousness which novels by "the author of *Waverley*" had been stimulating since 1814. So Scott was rightly put in charge of the proceedings and achieved a costume-piece which played from 15 to 29 August 1822 and turned out to be a smash-hit. The sixty-year-old monarch, arrayed in Royal Stuart tartan, was affable, enthusiastic and showed a fine sense of occasion. Many Scotsmen experienced a renewed sentiment of

Her Majesty in the Highlands.
A luncheon at Cairn Lochan, 1861

nationhood and a number of Lowlanders, in imitation of the First
Gentleman, began to affect the kilt, which was, for them, an
entirely new form of national dress. When George IV died in
1830 he was not universally lamented, but the laird of Abbotsford, already a sick man himself, mourned genuinely. He was,
however, comforted by his confident and unshaken belief in the
success of those August days whose memory remained undimmed
by the passage of eight years.

On 1 September 1842 Queen Victoria, accompanied by her
husband, Prince Albert of Saxe-Coburg, landed at Leith. It was
not long before the Royal pair had crossed the Highland Line
and within ten days they had both become "quite fond of the
bagpipes". And so there began that love-affair with Scotland of
which the Queen never wearied and whose monument is the holiday castle of Balmoral which Albert created. Here, in the tartan
decorated rooms and on the hill, was happiness – which the
Royal authoress recorded meticulously and skilfully in her diaries,
later published as *Leaves from the Journal of our Life in the Highlands*.
The Queen and her consort had founded a Scottish home which
their successors have maintained, the bond between the Royal
Family and Scotland became close and remained close – to be
delightfully strengthened in 1923 when the Duke of York, later
George VI, married Lady Elizabeth Bowes-Lyon, daughter of the
Earl of Strathmore.

THE CONDITION OF SCOTLAND

The great Queen might write of "this dear Paradise", but Victorian Scotland did not present a universally agreeable picture
either north or south of the Highland Line. The failure of the
potato crop, which caused the notorious Irish famine of 1846,
drove hundreds of Highlanders from their homes for lack of
food. There were further clearances between 1840 and 1854, not
without genuine desire to improve the economy, but in which the
creation of deer forests and other sporting amenities played their
part. Many of the victims of these misfortunes joined their compatriots overseas, many were sucked into the vortex of the Industrial Revolution, where they met immigrant Irish in like case.

For the wheels of the Industrial Revolution, already moving fast in the reign of George III, had continued to turn at a great pace. The start had been made with textiles – first linen, then cotton – but King Cotton was to be knocked off his Scottish throne by the American "War Between the States" of 1861–1865. A powerful successor, however, stood ready at hand. In 1801 the metallurgist David Mushet appreciated the economic value of black-band ironstone; in 1828 James Neilson, foreman of the Glasgow Gasworks, realized the potentialities of the hot blast-furnace. These two developments laid the foundations of the heavy industry upon which Scotland's fortunes were to be based until the end of the First World War. Railways proliferated, mighty iron vessels slid from the stocks on Clydeside and great ships of steel followed, once the Englishman, Henry Bessemer, had demonstrated to the British Association (1856) that this "Eldest Brother of Iron" could be produced infinitely more cheaply than had hitherto been the case. Fortunes were made at the expense of appalling suffering. Since Scottish miners had been bound, as serfs, to their work until 1799, it was not to be expected that early nineteenth-century manufacturers would conduct their concerns on high principles, even if Robert Owen had been practising them at the New Lanark Mills before the death of George IV. This

PASSENGER
TO CANADA

socialist reformer, who believed as strongly as any Arnoldian pedagogue in his ability to mould character, and who probably entertained more advanced views than most contemporary headmasters on humanity and lack of constraint, demonstrated that a good working environment – achieved by kindly if interfering paternalism – could be made to pay. New Lanark had many visitors, but few imitators. In fact it would be hard to find in other parts of the British Isles or Europe Industrial Revolution conditions as bad as those suffered by the Scots. Men, women and children faced long hours and hideous cruelty for low wages, in dangerous mines and bleak factories; they were ravaged in overcrowded tenements by cholera, smallpox, typhus and typhoid; many of their children took to crime and suffered brutal punishment – the mills were indeed satanic. However a measure of relief was brought by Factory and Mines legislation between 1833 and 1847, Trade Unionism began to influence the situation from 1850 onwards, in 1862 Scotland acquired a Medical Officer of Health and, by the 1880s, conditions had improved. But a deep bitterness had been engendered, which comes as no surprise to those who appreciate the realism of Euripides, and of the writer of Exodus XX, both of whom knew that the sins of the fathers are visited on the children.

The drift to the industrial areas and the flight overseas continued. Farming slumped as the century turned. World War I naturally provided a boost for heavy industry, now in decline. By 1918, two million persons out of a population of five million had gathered in the Glasgow area. The depression between the wars hit Scotland particularly hard, but since World War II, in common with the rest of Great Britain, she has become part of a welfare state, with an economy infinitely more varied than that of 1914. The miners are now less productive, but agriculture is healthier than it was, the fisheries are important and forestry proceeds apace. One may claim that heavy industry's downturn is being offset by electronics which are assisting the continued development of North Sea oil activities. Scottish based finance (banks and insurance companies) is also increasing employment and, though the whisky boom no longer obtains (Americans are allegedly spurning "the water of life"), sales should be helped by

Robert Owen by W. H. Brooke
(*Scottish National Portrait Gallery*)

the vast expansion of tourism, which stimulates not only the cult
of gastronomic specialities, the manufacture of tweeds and
tartans, but also a sophisticated programme of road building.
Although many parts of Scotland are particularly badly affected

by unemployment, urban aid schemes and development agencies are trying to alleviate its effects in inner cities, new towns and the countryside. A writer in the *Financial Times* has recently said: "One morning Scotland will wake to find things are not so bad".

"THE SPIRIT OF RAMBLING AND ADVENTURE"
(Smollett, *Humphry Clinker*)

Scotsmen were inveterate travellers long before the condition of their homeland forced them, in their thousands, into emigration. "The spirit of rambling and adventure has always been peculiar to the natives of Scotland," writes Smollett. "If they had not met with encouragement in England they would have served and settled as formerly, in other countries, such as Muscovy, Sweden, Denmark, Poland, Germany, France, Piedmont and Italy, in all which nations their descendants continue to flourish even at this day." (1777)

The armies, the universities and the markets of the continent had, indeed, long known the rambling and adventurous Scot. However rightly Sydney Smith, who edited the first number of *The Edinburgh Review* in 1802, might deplore the "passion for military glory", there is no doubt that the sword pays a bigger romantic dividend than does the scholar's gown or the pedlar's pack, and there had been a formidable tradition of Scotsmen soldiering in Europe before Quentin Durward joined the Scottish Archers of Louis XI's Guard. Among the high-ranking were Alexander Leslie under Gustavus Adolphus, George and James Keith at Potsdam and on the battlefields of Frederick the Great, and Alexandre Macdonald, whose father came from South Uist, serving Napoleon at Wagram and created Marshal of France.

The Hudson's Bay Company, founded in 1670 with the search for the Northwest Passage as one of its objects, employed many a Scottish adventurer. After the Union opportunities presented themselves in the Empire, later diplomacy proved an attraction and Henry Dundas started the tradition of his countrymen's service in India where they distinguished themselves as military men, civil servants and, indeed, proconsuls. Explorers have naturally captured the imagination: Mungo Park (from Selkirk) on

David Livingstone by E. Grimston
(*Scottish National Portrait Gallery*)

the Niger, David Livingstone (from Blantyre) in the African
interior. You have only to take down your atlas and look at place
names in Australia, New Zealand, the Pacific and Canada to
compile a Scottish Roll of Honour. But not all emigrants were as
successful as Andrew Carnegie (from Dunfermline) who reached
Pittsburgh in 1848, ended as a United States steel tycoon and
retired to his native heath to spend his declining years giving away
organs and endowing libraries – convinced, as he was, of the

wickedness of dying rich! Perhaps just as attractive to those who have sailed the Seven Seas and who know where "the old flotilla lay" is the humbler but ubiquitous figure of Kipling's "dour Scots engineer".

GODLINESS, GOOD LEARNING AND KINDRED SUBJECTS

It will be recalled that in the reign of William and Mary Presbyterianism was re-established in Scotland, with congregations once again choosing their own ministers – generally regarded as an essential characteristic of this way of religion. But in 1712 the lay patronage, which had caused so much trouble after the Restoration of Charles II (see page 166), was reintroduced. It was typical of the eighteenth century, when "moderate men looked big, Sir", that a Moderate party should have preponderance in the church and be prepared to accept this ruling. This party was one of real intellectual distinction – but it could not control a Popular element which staged two withdrawals during the next forty years, that of the Secession Church in 1734 and of the Relief Church in 1752. From about 1820 onwards what might be called the Evangelical opposition within the Church of Scotland was led by the formidable Dr Thomas Chalmers – mathematician, moral philosopher, educationist, theologian and divine – who, still in protest against lay patronage, led the great Disruption of 1843. At this juncture he departed with more than four hundred ministers to found the highly popular and successful Free Church of Scotland – which meant that there were now three important breakaways outside the establishment. However in 1874 the Patronage Act was repealed and, by various stages, the breakaways amalgamated. By 1929, with certain obstinately independent exceptions like the "Wee Frees", they were home once more and in the bosom of the Established Church. This church is organized into and regulated by (in ascending order of seniority) Kirk Sessions, Presbyteries, Synods and the General Assembly – each presided over by a Moderator. The Moderator of the General Assembly, elected for one year (called the "Right Reverend" while in office and the "Very Reverend" subsequently) enjoys

Thomas Chalmers by Sir D. Macnee
(*Scottish National Portrait Gallery*)

precedence in Scotland comparable with, though not precisely
the same as, that of the Archbishop of Canterbury in England.
The Queen, when unable to attend the General Assembly, is
represented by a Lord High Commissioner, whose office is an
annual Royal appointment.

Meanwhile the travelling Anglican will find that familiar
services, with a noble Liturgy dating back – with some revision

– to Charles I's Prayer Book of 1637, are offered by the Episcopal Church in Scotland. This is an independent ecclesiastical body, in communion with the Church of England, which traces its descent from the post-Restoration arrangements of the 1660s. Its subsequent Jacobite sympathies led to persecution under penal laws in the eighteenth century, but this unhappy state of affairs ended shortly after the death of Prince Charles Edward in 1788 when Jacobitism – a cause which could no longer be seriously sustained – faded into a world of nostalgia and romance. Today this branch of the church is led by seven bishops and has something over 46,000 communicant members.

Roman Catholicism has always survived in Scotland, for reforming ideas did not penetrate all areas of the Highlands and Islands.* An attractive modern monument to the persistence of the old faith is to be seen in Hew Lorimer's great statue of "Our Lady of the Isles" on South Uist, just as Glasgow's Roman Catholic Cathedral bears witness to the drift of Highlanders to that city before the influx of Irish immigrants in the second half of the nineteenth century. Under two archbishops and six bishops the Roman Communion in Scotland numbers some 760,000 souls.

Reference has been made more than once in this book to the Knoxian educational ideal, and it has been seen that neither this, nor the hopes raised by the act of 1696, had been achieved by the end of George III's reign. The progress which may be observed up to that time is largely attributable to the work of the Church of Scotland, which was later heavily reinforced by that of Dr Chalmers' Free Church, and to the efforts of the Society for the Propagation of Christian Knowledge – particularly in the Highlands. But the shift of population caused by the Industrial Revolution presented an educational problem beyond the scope of ecclesiastical organizations and religious bodies, with the result that the second half of the nineteenth century saw an alarming number of totally illiterate children. The state had to step in and the Education Act of 1892 made elementary education, financed by the ratepayers, universally available and compulsory. Today twelve education authorities, under the Scottish Education

* Readers of Dickens' *Barnaby Rudge* will remember the "Gordon Riots", provoked by the Catholic Relief Act of 1778.

Department, bear responsibility for this vital activity and, in the 1960s the universities of Strathclyde (1964), Heriot-Watt, Edinburgh (1966), Dundee and Stirling (1967) took their places beside the ancient foundations of St Andrews, Glasgow, Aberdeen and Edinburgh.

An assessment of contemporary culture in Scotland does not fall within the scope of this book, but it seems generally agreed that after the death of Sir Walter Scott in 1832 and of James Hogg, the great Selkirkshire peasant-poet, in 1835, the glories of the eighteenth–nineteenth-century "hot-bed of genius" faded. Of course there was Thomas Carlyle, from Ecclefechan, but he moved to Cheyne Walk in 1834, and there was Robert Louis Stevenson, driven from his home by tuberculosis to die in Samoa in 1894 – but it is perhaps too early to judge the extent to which the works of subsequent authors will stand the test of time. There is certainly abundant evidence that modern Scotland is culturally enormously alive – the Edinburgh Festival, the work of the Scottish Arts Council, the Burrell Collection, the theatre in the capital, in Glasgow, Dundee and Perth, at St Andrews and at Pitlochry demonstrate this, but it is difficult to judge (except in the, to many of us obscure, matter of Gaelic literature) the extent to which this activity is specifically Scottish, British or even European.

*   *   *

Almost two hundred years ago Smollett wrote: "the contempt for Scotland which prevails too much on this side of the Tweed, is founded on prejudice and error". Today, when on average 4·5 million* holiday makers visit Scotland annually, the picture is very different. Those of us who can do so treasure any tea-spoonful of Scottish blood to which we may lay claim. We experience a sense of excitement when we cross the Border, for we know that, despite the standardization which menaces the period in which we live, we have come into what the Scottish Tourist Board calls "a world of a difference".

* Figures supplied by the Scottish Tourist Board.

INDEX